CAMBRIDGE STUDIES IN PHILOSOPHY

The Engines of the Soul

T0381657

CAMBRIDGE STUDIES IN PHILOSOPHY

General *editor* SYDNEY SHOEMAKER

Advisory *editors* J. E. J. ALTHAM, SIMON BLACKBURN,
GILBERT HARMAN, MARTIN HOLLIS, FRANK JACKSON,
JONATHAN LEAR, JOHN PERRY, HARRY STROUD

The Engines of
the Soul

W. D. Hart

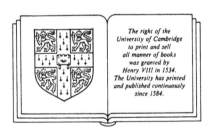

The right of the
University of Cambridge
to print and sell
all manner of books
was granted by
Henry VIII in 1534.
The University has printed
and published continuously
since 1584.

Cambridge University Press

Cambridge
New York   New Rochelle   Melbourne   Sydney

CAMBRIDGE UNIVERSITY PRESS
Cambridge, New York, Melbourne, Madrid, Cape Town, Singapore, São Paulo, Delhi

Cambridge University Press
The Edinburgh Building, Cambridge CB2 8RU, UK

Published in the United States of America by Cambridge University Press, New York

www.cambridge.org
Information on this title: www.cambridge.org/9780521107693

First published 1988
This digitally printed version 2009

A catalogue record for this publication is available from the British Library

Library of Congress Cataloguing in Publication data
Hart, W. D. (Wilbur Dyre), 1943–
The engines of the soul.
(Cambridge studies in philosophy)
Includes index.
1. Dualism. 2. Mind and body. 3. Causation.
I. Title. II. Series
B812.H37   1988   128'.2   87-32648

ISBN 978-0-521-34290-2 hardback
ISBN 978-0-521-10769-3 paperback

In memory of my parents

Contents

Preface

If you are holding this book in your hand, your mind is lodged in a body. Neither your mind nor your body is more basic than the other; either could exist even if the other did not. There could be a disembodied person reading this book over your shoulder right now. This view is, or is like a version of, Descartes's dualism. The best argument for this view is also due to Descartes: what you can imagine is possible, and you can imagine being disembodied, so you could be disembodied.

Since the seventeenth century, the question of causal interaction between things as different as mind and matter has presented a problem, perhaps the leading problem, for dualism. This is as much a problem about the nature of causation as it is about mind and matter, and a treatment of it can be ranged under argument for the second premise of Descartes's argument, namely, that you can imagine being disembodied. As we shall work that premise out, it issues in a form of Cartesian dualism less like Descartes's own view than like the folklore of ghosts. We may be trapped poltergeists.

Such views may be naïve, primitive, or even unscientific. But it would be something else to think that they offend common sense. To be sure, since World War II one kind of materialism or another seems to have been orthodox among professional analytic philosophers who specialize in the philosophy of mind. For the first two decades or so after the war, a time dominated by the epistemic problem of other minds, something like behaviorism was orthodox, whereas in the past two decades, a time dominated by the metaphysi-

cal mind–body problem, one kind of central state materialism or another has become orthodox. This seems like an
unstable consensus in a small group. For at least two millennia, some sort of dualism has been orthodox among at least
Europeans and may still be a strand of common sense (especially grounded in a claim of possibility). It would seem harsh
to call that view bizarre or preposterous, especially when
there is a valid argument for it from true premises.

A friend and colleague warns that this book will be hated
because it is so contrary to the spirit of the age. Anyone
whose opinions are unorthodox should take care that he or
she is not out merely to *épater les bourgeois;* that motive is too
adolescent. But orthodoxy needs devil's advocates; they have
a serious part in the play of ideas even if committed heterodoxy invites excommunication. Another friend and former
colleague once published an intriguing challenge to a logical
orthodoxy that drew three replies, each one satisfied of its
own conclusiveness; it made him think he was on to something that any two of these conclusive replies were inconsistent with each other.

Philosophers at Columbia University, Trinity College
Dublin, and University College London heard earlier ver-
sions of some of these pages and their reflections were help-
ful. In earlier days Graham Curtis's insightful conversation
was supportive, as was Malcolm Budd's later on; Richard
Wollheim created a department that encouraged serious
thought untrammeled by narrow conventions or intellectual
piety. Wendy Robins is owed thanks for making words in-
carnate, as is Cambridge University Press for having the
services of Jonathan Sinclair-Wilson; philosophy is well
served by an editor of intelligence, taste, and firm tact, without whom heterodoxy might never see the dark of print.
The argument in these pages was honed against the acute
and thoughtful criticism of the general editor of this series,
Professor Sydney Shoemaker, and of an earlier reader

whom anonymity shields from being thanked by name. Mary Nevader's careful editing has polished the prose. Faith and Luke Hart know what these pages cost, and paid not a little of the price themselves. But I am responsible for my apostasy and its errors.

1

The problem

Are you lodged in your body, or indeed any body, only by accident? Or is it absolutely necessary not only that you be lodged in some body or other, but also that you have the specific body you now inhabit? Asking these two questions is one way to raise what is known as the mind–body problem: how are you related to your body? How is the mind (the self, the person) related to matter?

Descartes is famous for, among other things, his dualist solution to the mind–body problem. Mind–body dualism is the thesis that there are at least two basic or fundamental sorts of things: one including you and other minds, selves, or persons, and the other including the bodies of you and other people as well as inanimate lumps of matter like stars, planets, and glaciers. Things that are basic or fundamental are sometimes called substances. In this usage, a substance is not a stuff (like sugar or air) but a basic or fundamental thing. That understood, we could restate mind–body dualism as the thesis that you (or anyone else) and your body (or anyone else's) are two different substances.

What does it mean to call a thing basic or fundamental? The central idea is that a basic thing exists independently, that is, that it is not dependent for its existence on the existence of anything else. This is in turn an idea about what is possible, not about what is actually true. For example, an electron or a quark is in the relevant way basic if it is possible that it should exist even if nothing else existed. Consider any object apart from the particle and ask whether the particle could have existed even if the other object did not; if the answer is always

1

yes, then the particle is a basic thing and thus a substance. Note that you are not to ask whether the other object you consider in fact fails to exist; since that object was there for you to consider, that question would always be answered by a trivial no. Rather, you are to ask whether the electron could still have existed even if the other object had not. So whether a thing is a substance is a question about possibility.

Could stars, planets, or glaciers exist without the bits (like electrons) making them up or without the events (like condensations of nebulae or ice ages with their constituent objects) that formed those stars, planets, and glaciers? Someone like Leibniz, thinking about the first question, might wonder whether only things like fundamental particles are substances. Someone like Spinoza, thinking about the second question, might wonder whether only the universe as a whole is a substance. Partly because it seems naturally to lead to such widely divergent speculations, the concept of a substance is no longer so taken for granted as it once was.

But the concept of a substance does not seem to lead to such difficulties in the mind–body problem. Using that concept, we may state the crux of dualism as the thesis that you and all other minds, selves, and persons are substances. This means that you and other persons are basic things, which means that you and other people are not dependent for your existence on the existence of any other objects. But in asking whether people depend for their existence on something else, it is clear that the other objects of which we are thinking primarily are people's bodies. So the question becomes: could you exist even if your body did not? Could you be disembodied? We need no suspicious concept of substance to ask that question.

For some time the prevailing orthodoxy has been that dualism is false and that you could not be disembodied. This view has in recent decades been connected with theses about identity. First, it is argued that you (or your mental states) are identical with your brain (or states of your central nervous system). But, second, things cannot be identical only by accident; properly understood, all true identities are necessary truths. Hence, your mental states are necessarily identical with electrochemical states of your central system, and thus you could not exist unless (at least part of) your body did. Since you could not be disembodied, dualism is false.

The core of this argument is that people are identical with their bodies, so since identities are necessary, people could not be disembodied, and thus dualism is false. That is, if people are identical with their bodies, then dualism is false. Hence, dualism requires that people not be identical with their bodies. But, and this is the present point, dualism requires more than that people are not identical with their bodies. Clench your left hand and look at your left fist. It might at first seem plausible to say that your left fist is identical with your left hand. But identical things should have all their properties in common; and in particular, when things are identical with each other, they should exist at the same times. Yet if you now open your left hand, your left fist is gone, though your left hand remains. Thus, your left hand and your left fist do not exist at the same times; so they are not identical. (As it were, your left fist is your left hand clenched, and your left hand clenched is your left hand in a certain state, not your left hand *tout court*.) But although hand–fist identity is false, a hand–fist dualism would seem decidedly heroic; it is too much to believe that your left fist could exist even if your left hand did not. This suggests by analogy what might be called mentalism, that is, that although you (or your mind or self) are not identical with your body (or even with a part of it like your central nervous system, even the electrochemical states now obtaining in that system), still you could not be disembodied. The point is that mind–body dualism is stronger than mind–body difference, for mentalism asserts difference but denies the possibility of disembodiment, whereas dual-

3

ism asserts difference because it asserts the possibility of disembodiment. The mentalist denies that the mind is a substance, whereas the dualist asserts that it is.

Your mind is a substance if it is not dependent for its existence on that of your body. It is important to understand that the relevant sort of dependence is a matter of necessity, not natural law. To illustrate the difference, as a matter presumably of natural law there have been stallions as long as there have been mares, and vice versa. Still, it seems clear that Aristotle, to whom the notion of a substance is due, would have counted both mares and stallions among the (primary) substances; each could exist without the other, as we know because we can imagine there being mares but no stallions, and vice versa. It thus seems better to explain substance in terms of possibility *simpliciter* rather than so-called natural possibility; one thing is independent of another if the first could exist but the other not, even if that would violate contingent natural law.

It is worthwhile to see clearly how very strong a thesis dualism is because in that way one begins to see how much a good argument for dualism should establish. But Descartes's argument for dualism, although it is strong, is also simple. Other things being equal, simple philosophical arguments are preferable to subtle arguments. In a field like mathematics, the craftsmen know, at least more or less, the state of the art. For that reason, subtle mathematical arguments may carry the day; where the craftsman knows the state of the art, he can reasonably expect to survey all possibilities. But even the best philosophical craftsmen seem never to master the state of their art fully; indeed, it may never in the relevant sense have a full state. For that reason, subtlety is, other things being equal, suspect in philosophical arguments.

Descartes's argument for dualism has two premises. The first premise is not especially about the nature of the mind, but about evidence for possibility: it says that what you can imagine is possible. The second premise says that you can imagine being disembodied. It is the second premise that turns out, on examination, to say a great deal about the nature of the mind. The argument is that from these two premises, dualism follows; that is, it follows that you could be disembodied, which consequence is the central thesis of dualism.

Philosophical habit puts an argument to two questions in order. First, one asks whether the argument is valid; forgetting about whether the premises and the conclusion are true or false, one asks whether the conclusion follows from the premises. Are the premises such that if they were true, the conclusion would also be true? The second premise of Descartes's argument may be stated slightly more explicitly as

(2) You can imagine that you should be disembodied.

Similarly, the first premise of the argument could be stated as

(1) If you can imagine that p, then it is possible that p,

where the letter 'p' marks two blanks that could be filled by almost any sentence in the indicative mood (but that for grammatical purposes should then be shifted into something like the subjunctive mood). If we fill these two blanks with the indicative sentence "You are disembodied," we get

(3) If you can imagine that you should be disembodied, then it is possible that you should be disembodied.

The idea is that a commitment to Descartes's first premise requires for just about any indicative sentence S a commitment to the result of filling the two blanks in (1) by S; so (3) follows from Descartes's first premise. From (2) and (3) we deduce

(4) It is possible that you should be disembodied.

Our conclusion, (4), is deduced from (2) and (3) by a logical principle called *modus ponens*: suppose that A; and that if A, then B; then B. *Modus ponens* is a principle of reasoning the soundness of which cannot be faulted. In sum, then, Descartes's logic cannot be faulted; and if you can imagine being disembodied, it follows that you could be disembodied. (It is a virtue of simpler philosophical arguments that one is more likely to be able to judge their validity sensibly.)

Once a philosophical argument has satisfied the canons of validity, habit then asks whether its premises are true. Here we encounter something like a historical oddity. It would seem that to Descartes and to many people before him, but to fewer and fewer people since the seventeenth century, it was just plain obvious both that what is imaginable is possible and that being disembodied is imaginable. But most educated and thoughtful late-twentieth-century audiences refuse to accept Descartes's premises without further argument. It is the purpose of what follows to attempt to push the argument for those premises back to further premises that a twentieth-century audience could accept.

This pushing argument backward is a kind of philosophical exploration, and it is an exploration that decidedly does not leave Descartes's dualism unchanged. As we explore, the feel or *Gestalt* of Cartesian dualism will change radically but inevitably from the dualism of Descartes's original text; so the reader should be asking himself constantly whether the altering prize is still genuine mind–body dualism.

But there remains the historical question why what seemed obvious, that you can imagine being disembodied, in the seventeenth century and before has since seemed less and less obvious. It could be that people's imaginations have grown increasingly dimmer over the past three hundred or so years; but it might be too self-serving to take this suggestion very seriously. A more orthodox explanation might appeal to two factors: the decline of Christian faith and the successes of natural science. (It is a matter of some sensitivity whether these two factors are independent, but that, fortunately, is not a question we need answer here.) As for the first factor, there seems traditionally to have been at least an association of ideas between the immateriality of the mind and the im-

6

mortality of the soul. Joseph Addison, for example, clearly associates immateriality and immortality in the first two paragraphs of Number 111 of the *Spectator*.[1] With the decline of Christian faith, belief in the immortal soul seems increasingly like wishful thinking. Putting away childish things, one ceases to be able to take a wishful belief in immortality seriously; it becomes a test of independent pride to deny the life ever after. To the extent that immaterial minds are mixed up with immortal souls, it also becomes a measure of clearheaded adulthood that one deny the immaterial mind and one's capacity to imagine being disembodied.

Belief in the possibility of disembodiment is not exclusive to Christians, so a defender of dualism should not have to defend Christianity. Nevertheless, there will turn out to be an intriguing linkage of ideas underpinning Addison's association between immateriality and immortality. Is this link necessary? We will thus ask eventually whether disembodied people could nonetheless die.

The second factor, the rise of natural science, seems to have worked against the immaterial mind in something like the following fashion. For about three hundred years, more and more natural processes have yielded up their secrets to human understanding, and some of them have yielded up their working to our control, apparently by being conquered through the working hypothesis that they are physical engines driven by lifeless natural forces. That the hypothesis has worked so often and so spectacularly is a reason for believing that it is true. It is then only natural to generalize, that is, to suppose that all natural phenomena, including people ourselves, are at bottom nothing but physical engines driven by electrochemical forces. To deny the application of materialism to ourselves seems to be like standing with the churchmen refusing to look through Galileo's telescope, with the bishop of Oxford when T. H. Huxley made a fool of him, with Joseph Breuer when his offended dignity prevented him from pursuing with Freud the psychosexual mysteries in the uncon-

7

scious, and with the Nazi officials who proscribed Einstein's "Jewish" physics. To keep such company willingly is to cast oneself on the rubbish pile of history.

It has been patent ever since the seventeenth century that the problem of how disembodiable minds could interact causally with any matter at all, not just the bodies in which those minds might somehow happen to be lodged, is a (if not the) central intellectual problem for Cartesian dualists. The usual verdict seems to have been to throw up one's intellectual hands in despair and to claim that the mental is the physical. But despairful thinking is no better than wishful thinking; on appeal, that verdict should receive the Scottish judgment: not proven. No identity between your belief that there are infinitely many prime numbers and some state of your central nervous system has ever been exhibited. The price paid for a despairful belief that the mind is the brain ticking over has been an absence of intellectual experiment, that is, an absence of sustained and informed speculation about how disembodiable minds could engage in causal transactions with matter. In a sense, materialists do not know what they are denying; if they wished to be charitable, they might suppose that they are about to be told one version of what they deny.[2]

2

The knowledge of possibility

The first premise of Descartes's argument was the principle that what can be imagined is possible; as Hume later put it, ". . . nothing we imagine is absolutely impossible."[1] This should not in the first instance be construed as a metaphysical principle stating the nature of possibility. Although it states that imaginability suffices for possibility, it does not state the reverse, that is, that possibility suffices for imaginability; in the jargon of philosophical logic, one would say that the principle states a sufficient condition for possibility, not a necessary condition. Imagining that such and such is one way to learn that it is possible that such and such; there may be others. (Since anything actual is possible, knowledge of an actuality that you cannot imagine, like a quantum mechanical wavicle perhaps or curved space-time, yields knowledge of possibility you cannot imagine; so inability to imagine a possibility must yield to theoretical inference from perception of its actuality.) But an analysis of the nature of possibility should state a condition necessary and sufficient for possibility. Moreover, the condition that the principle states as sufficient for possibility is itself a condition of possibility, that is, that it *can* be imagined that such and such. So were the principle construed as an analysis of the nature of possibility, it would be viciously circular.

The interest of the principle is rather more epistemological than metaphysical; it points at a sort of evidence to which we appeal in justifying claims about what could be the case or what must be the case, claims called modal after the modal auxilliaries "can" and "must." As an epistemological principle, it seems to be connected by an analogy with traditional empiricism. At the core of empiricism lies the doctrine that perception is the basic faculty we exercise in justifying beliefs about what is actually true. The analogy is that as perception justifies (some) belief in actual truth, so imagination justifies (some) belief in possible truth; perception is to the actual as imagination is to the possible.

Of course, if empiricism is to allow that we know more than the things we can observe to be true one by one, if, that is, empiricism is to allow us knowledge of or justification for scientific theory, then it must concede perhaps less perceptual, more intellectual faculties in the exercise of which theory is tested against, and justified by, observed data. An epistemology for modal belief should perhaps allow for similar, or perhaps even the same, intellectual faculties. But perception seems to be the single recognized mode of intercourse with actual objects, the subject matter of beliefs, whereby we acquire information about them that justifies beliefs about the actual world; so if we are to be justified in believing that scientific theory is true of the actual world, the justification of that belief must be grounded in perception in order that theoretical belief make contact with the actual world.

One wants to say that knowledge of possibility should be grounded in imagination for the same reason that theoretical knowledge about actuality should be grounded in perception of actual objects. But here we confront an antinomy that may explain the perennial philosophical interest in modality. The antinomy is that what would seem necessary to make objective modal truth possible also makes justified modal knowledge impossible.[2]

Consider, first, objective truth. It is, we think, an objective truth that the moon revolves about the earth. This truth is objective, it seems, because whether we believe it or not, whether we like it or not, there are out there in space two enormous rocks, the moon and the earth, the one swinging about the other. That is, the independent existence of objects

10

in a proposition's (sentence's, thought's, statement's; which does not matter) subject matter seems to make for its objective truth. Since one is hard pressed to come up with any alternative route to objective truth, it is hard to deny that the independent existence of objects in the subject matter of a sentence is also necessary for the objective truth of that sentence; in order that a sentence be an objective truth about its subject matter, that subject matter should exist independently of whether we are aware of it. Leibniz introduced for modal truth the picture of possible worlds; the idea is that a sentence that is not actually true nonetheless could be true if and only if there exists a possible world in which it is true. This picture was revived in the 1950s and has been considerably elaborated since then. It pushes us toward the result that objective modal truth requires the independent existence of nonactual, possible worlds in addition to this, the actual world.

Many people seem to find this result rebarbative. The strongest ground for their distaste is epistemic. Suppose that imagination is to knowledge of possibility as perception is to knowledge of actuality. As we shall see, perception is essentially and necessarily a causal transaction; perceiving an object yields knowledge of it only because one acquires information about it in a causal transaction with it. So if imagination is to yield knowledge of other possible worlds analogously to the way perception yields knowledge of this world, then imagination would seem to have to involve a causal transaction between us in this, the actual world, and nonactual, imagined objects in other, objectively real, possible worlds. But it is a metaphysical axiom that there can be causal transactions only between denizens of a single world, that causal signals cannot pass from unactualized possibilia to actualia, that the limits of a single world are fixed by its possible causal interactions. Independently existing possible worlds seem to be required for objective modal truth, but also to make modal knowledge impossible. (The form of this antinomy, a conflict between the metaphysical demands of objective truth and the episte-

11

mological demands on knowledge of the required objects, is shared by several philosophical problems.)

How might one respond to this dilemma? One might say that knowledge of possibilia never resembles perception of actual objects like stones, but resembles theoretical knowledge of objects like electrons or numbers. That is, you know that there are electrons and numbers, not because you see them, but because you need to suppose them in order best to explain what you do observe; and that is a good reason for thinking that electrons and numbers exist. But such an account would work only if we needed unactualized possibilia in order best to explain what we observe; and it is by no means clear that natural science needs to suppose unactualized possibilia in order to explain observed phenomena. To be sure, Fermat's principle of least time explains the observed law of reflection by the claim that among all possible routes a light ray might take from an object to a mirror and thence to an observer, the one in which the angle of incidence equals the angle of reflection is the path of extremal (here, least) time. But those other unactualized possible paths of the light ray are actual curves in space; as Isaiah Berlin noted some years ago,[3] we are the more comfortable with unactualized possibilities the more firmly they are rooted in actual things, even comparatively abstract actual things like geometric objects. Hence, some possibilia are admitted to scientific explanations, but only by identification with actual abstract denizens of this world; and insofar as knowledge of possibilia is knowledge of actual abstracta, that knowledge is no more problematic than mathematical knowledge. But advocates of possible-worlds realism usually distinguish those worlds from abstract objects actual in this world, and it remains to be shown that other worlds and their denizens are needed in scientific explanations of phenomena in this world. (Indeed, to the extent that explanations trace causes but nonactual, possible concreta cannot influence actual objects causally, it is hard to see how scientific explanations could need possibilia;

but this point must be taken with a grain of salt, since science does need causally inert abstract objects.) Then, too, likening knowledge of possibilia to knowledge of numbers seems false to the phenomenology of modal knowledge. That is, in many cases it seems to be the exercise of the imagination that produces conviction in modal beliefs. Since the analogy with knowledge of numbers leaves no role for the imagination, it does not fit the experience of acquiring modal belief.

One might respond to the dilemma with a kind of modal idealism. That is, just as the idealist Bishop Berkeley said that to be is to be perceived and the material objects are collections of our ideas, so also one might say that the visual images you form when you imagine do not represent possibilities that exist independently of your representations of them, but that those images just are unactualized possibilities. On this view, modal knowledge is a kind of self-knowledge; and modal truth is no more fixed than the truth about you. The most serious difficulty in this modal idealism is that, like any idealism, it threatens the objectivity of a species of truths. There will be no more fact of a modal matter than the range of imaginings about it that we have managed so far; were our imaginations crippled or enhanced tomorrow, the modal facts would change. Possibility was born with us and will die with us. One response, perhaps Quine's, is to conclude that modality is all a delusion and to be outgrown when one gives up the metaphysics of childhood or the stone age. Such disillusion costs dearly; for the mind–body problem, the question of dualism, is a modal question. So if there is no objective modal truth, there is no modal fact of the matter about whether dualism is true or false. One might come to a commitment to materialism as strong as Quine's partly by disillusion with modality and thus the legitimacy of the mind–body problem.

If one thinks that the mind–body problem is a real problem with a correct answer and thus is not willing to accept Quine's disillusion, and if one nonetheless cannot solve the dilemma (if, for example, one cannot accept causal transactions between different possible worlds), then it is hard to see any alternative to hope. What can one do but insist that knowable, objective modal truth must be possible and hope that someone will someday explain how it is possible? Forlorn as that hope is, nothing better is evident.

Suppose, then, that objective modal truths can be known. The imagination is a faculty by which we acquire such convictions. Could there be a polar bear colored purple? Certainly, we say, because we can visualize a polar bear over whom purple dye has been poured. (A mutant purple polar bear would require more imaginative work in order to ensure that the mutation really is possible.) All those who have taken necessity seriously have been certain that there could not be an object that is simultaneously red all over and green all over. We know, presumably by observation, that no actual object happens to be simultaneously red all over and green all over. But as Kant wrote, experience teaches that a thing is so-and-so, not that it cannot be otherwise;[4] there is no such thing as an experience of necessity. So why are we so certain that there *could* not be an object simultaneously red all over and green all over? What seems to produce the conviction is one's inability to visualize such an object. One's own experience in settling modal questions seems to show that the imagination plays a fundamental role.

It is important to note that it is the inability to *visualize* an object red all over and green all over that convinces that such objects are impossible. That is, it is fundamentally sensory imagination that is to belief about possibility as perception is to belief about actuality. There are modes of imagination corresponding to each of the five senses; most of us can visualize, and although in many people the olfactory, gustatory, and tactual dimensions of imagination seem not as well developed, most of us can hear tunes in our heads. It is by virtue of the sensory character of these basic modes of imagination that

14

they sustain modal convictions in analogy with the way the five senses sustain beliefs about the actual world.

There are those who disdain the sensory imagination in favor of what seems to be a more intellectual faculty. This is sometimes called conception or conceiving; some scholars believe that Descartes himself founded modal knowledge in conceiving rather than in the sensory imagination. There is, indeed, an intellectual faculty, entertaining propositions (which is akin to understanding sentences), which is thoroughly intellectual, and which has no necessary sensory component. The successful exercise of this faculty gives, however, no evidence whatsoever of possibility. For we must be able to entertain propositions that could not possibly be true in order to be able to follow *reductio ad absurdum* proofs that they could not possibly be true. So the advocate of conception must be able to find a faculty intermediate between the sensory imagination and entertaining propositions. It must be intellectual, like the second, not sensory, like the first (though why the advocate should want this is obscure); but its successful exercise should yield evidence for possibility, in which respect it must be like the first, not the second. No such intermediate faculty seems to exist; introspection reveals none. So since it seems to be by virtue of the involuntary sensory limits on what we can sensorially imagine that the sensory imagination sustains modal conviction (and especially convictions of impossibility), it seems sensible to place one's modal faith more in sensory imagination than in conception. (This faith is compatible with recognizing that we may place intellectual constructions on foundations in the sensory imagination, much as we theorize in natural science on perceptual foundations.)

A leading idea of an epistemology of modality grounded in the sensuous imagination is an analogy between imagination and perception: as perception is to knowledge of the actual world, so imagination is to knowledge of other possible worlds. It is characteristic of perception that it can go wrong;

when a person hallucinates, he does not in fact perceive what it seems to him he perceives. A sensible epistemology for modality grounded in the imagination should doubtless allow for analogous infelicities. Hobbes, for example, is notorious for having thought he had imagined a procedure whereby any angle can be trisected using straightedge and compasses; but Hobbes's imaginings were, as it were, fuzzy, and Galois explained why no such procedure is to be imagined. We have no more privileged access to whether we have imagined a procedure for trisecting any angle than to whether we have perceived a perpetual motion machine. (Similarly, only slackness will allow one to think one has imagined a complete and consistent axiomatization of number theory, and Gödel explained why any detailed effort to do so will fail.)

The procedures by which fallible imagination is tested resemble those by which fallible perception is tested. If in doubt, one is wise to examine carefully what one seems to perceive and to try to bring others to perceive what one seems to perceive; declarations that what seems otherwise veridical perception is in fact illusory are more convincing given an explanation of why it is not perception but illusion. Similarly, in contentious cases, one should imagine in thorough detail in order to avoid overlooking a hidden hitch, and one should articulate a recipe whereby others can imagine what one has imagined. Declarations that what seems veridical imagining is illusory are more convincing given an explanation of why one has not really imagined what one seems to have imagined.

For example, some science fiction stories may seem to be recipes whereby one can imagine time travel. But so long as the laws of nature could then remain otherwise as they are, the time traveler could then kill his younger self before he sets off on his time travels. Since it is easy to miss this sort of hitch or paradox, at least on first reading a time-travel story, it is all too easy to think that one can really imagine time travel. But since further and more careful imagining reveals a hitch, it is not sensible to be sure that one can imagine time travel and thus that it really is possible; for here the paradox seems to be an explanation of why time travel is not to be imagined.

Some ask whether M. C. Escher depicted impossibilities. But they should try to put into words some of what Escher drew and ask whether it is impossible that this be true. For example, in *Relativity* we see part of a world with what seem to be three mutually perpendicular gravitational fields. Because it is an etching and thus, unlike a film, static, it is unclear whether these fields do not overlap or overlap without adding. This violates natural law, but one might say that Escher shows us evidence (but partly because it is static, only evidence, not proof) that it is not impossible. It is also interesting that there are only three mutually perpendicular fields. The idea of *Print Gallery* is something like a knot, that is, the way the space of the gallery is to loop round to become the space of a picture in the gallery. Note that at the center, where the knot should close, Escher drew a blank. *Belvedere* is a comment on the *conventions* of perspective in flat drawings; do the columns *look* vertical? One looking at *Ascending and Descending* or *Waterfall* should, like one looking at *Relativity*, ask whether the higher-than relation is necessarily transitive and irreflexive.[5]

We asked earlier how the imagination could justify objective modal knowledge. To ask how we might be justified in trusting the modal deliverances of the imagination is not yet to impugn those verdicts; a process can work even if we cannot understand how it can work. What would impugn the modal verdicts of the imagination? Would an antinomy, that is, a pair of propositions each firmly grounded in the imagination and equally so, but nonetheless inconsistent with each other, suffice? Is the following such an antinomy?

The first horn of the dilemma is that there could be only finitely many physical objects. Suppose there were infinitely many physical objects. Then it would seem too heroic to deny that there could be a countably infinite sequence of physical objects each after the first half the size of its immediate predecessor. But then Benardete's book, a book with infinitely many pages each after the first half as thick as its immediate predecessor, ought also to be possible.[6] Yet there is no imagining such a book. Turn it over and open the back cover; what would it look like? *Ex hypothesi* there is no last page to be seen. The imagination here draws a blank, much like the blank it draws when asked to visualize a cloth at once red all over and green all over. But if we thus have reason to believe that Benardete's book is impossible, that seems also to give us reason to believe that there could not be infinitely many physical objects.

It is already embarrassing that simply by imagining, we seem to be able to learn that there is a finite limit to the number of physical objects. But the other horn of the dilemma is that there could be infinitely many physical objects. Three-dimensional space could be infinitely large. This is not immediate; one does not visualize an infinite extent all at one go. But we seem to be able to extrapolate. Picture as much of a plane as you can, and imagine it marked off by a grid like Cartesian coordinates. It may be that the region that you can take in fuzzes out toward, say, a hundred units from the origin. So now imagine moving back far enough to shift the old fuzzy edge toward your center of vision. Now perhaps it may be more difficult to make discriminations as fine as before, but neither does the view begin to fuzz out until, say, a thousand units from the origin. Since there is no evident need for an end to such shifts backward, we become convinced that an infinite Euclidean plane is possible. If there were three such, each perpendicular to the other two (one before you, one beside, and one below), three-dimensional space would be infinitely large. But if three-dimensional space could be infinitely large, there is no evident reason that there could not be stars, say, at each of its points with integer coordinates. (Indeed, Newton argued that the universe is rather like that.)[7] In that case, there would be infinitely many physical objects.

It is contradictory to say both that there could be infinitely many physical objects and that there could not be; yet though neither modal claim is immediate, both seem fairly firmly grounded in the imagination. That is the antinomy.

How might one respond to this antinomy? With no serious claim to exhaustiveness, the following alternatives present themselves. More conservatively, one might fault the reasoning toward one (or both) horns of the dilemma. Of these, the first seems somehow more suspect. In the argument for the first horn, the inference from the possibility of an infinity of physical objects to the possibility of a countably infinite sequence of physical objects each after the first half the size of its immediate predecessor could be blocked if, among physical objects, there is a positive size below which they cannot fall; if, that is, there were in that sense a necessary minimum to the size of a physical object. But such a claim seems false: Visualize a sphere, or some other shape, of close to that size. Since it has a positive size, it should have a left and a right side, and it is thus easy to picture the object chopped in two, an object of size less than the supposed necessary minimum thus being produced. Necessary minima seem all too clearly to fail.

There might seem to be a hint of circularity in the argument for the second horn; for how does one know one can always move back from something unless one already knows there is endless space into which one could move back? It would block the argument for the second horn to claim that there is a distance from something beyond which one cannot imagine being. But this claim seems as clearly to fail as necessary minima.

For all one knows, someone might claim that the antinomy shows nothing about the imagination and modal knowledge, but is instead yet another paradox of the infinite. But in the absence of any such "solution" worked out, we are unable to evaluate the claim.

The first two responses force on us metaphysical results we

are unable to believe. Is there a more epistemological response to the antinomy? Most radically, one might deny that the imagination provides trustworthy grounds for claims of possibility and necessity. But since our beliefs about what is possible conform best to what we can imagine true and since there is no other such reasonable epistemology of modality in the offing, the present alternative verges on denying that there is objective modal knowledge. Perhaps so radical a result ought to be a conclusion of last resort.

The underdetermination of (nonmodal) theory by (perceptual) data, a commonplace of recent epistemology, entails that theories incompatible with each other may be equally well confirmed by all observation and better confirmed than any other theory. A commitment to the objectivity of modal truth, that is, to its independence from the way it seems to us, might lead one to expect that modal propositions could be similarly underdetermined by imaginative data. In that way, the present antinomy could be taken as a case in point.

Of all these responses, the last seems least disruptive; it tames the antinomy by assimilating it to a recognized pattern in nonmodal epistemology, thus extending the analogy between imagination and perception. So since the sensible response to theories underdetermined by data would seem to be suspension of judgment, in the face of our antinomy we should suspend judgment about whether there could be an infinity of physical objects.

Descartes's argument for dualism is an argument for a possibility, not for a necessity. For that reason, we have emphasized the role of imagination in establishing possibility rather than necessity. But it might be worthwhile to make a few remarks about how imagining can justify belief in necessary truth. In the first place, it will not do simply to say that what you cannot imagine to be false is necessarily true. If it is to be believed, twentieth-century physics is replete with truths you cannot imagine. A motivation for grounding modal knowledge in the sensory imagination is desire for an epistemology of modality as conformable as possible to the legitimate heirs of traditional empiricism. So our first attempt might be weakened to the principle that *truths* you cannot imagine to be false are necessary truths. This principle should be regarded as a principle of inference to the best explanation. That is, you have reason to believe necessary a truth whose necessity is the best explanation of your inability to imagine that it be false. The point of taking it as such a principle of inference is that we should wish to confine the inference to the necessity of a truth to those cases where you cannot imagine its denial because of something intrinsic to the nature of its subject matter and to exclude those cases where you cannot imagine a very complex denial simply because its complexity exceeds the capacities of, let us suppose, all finite imaginations.

You must, of course, try to imagine the denial, and you must exert all your ingenuity in doing so; it is only if you always fail in the attempt, and if you do not fail just because of your limitations rather than the nature of your subject, that your failures are good evidence that the truth is necessary. And even good evidence is short of conclusive proof. Suppose it is true that p and that for centuries after it was discovered that p, many bright people tried hard to imagine that not p, but never hit on a way to do so. They would then have good evidence that it is necessary that p. Nevertheless, it remains possible that there is a way it could be false that p, and that after those centuries, an inventive genius imagine a way it could be false that p. But this is no more than the old lesson that there are no guarantees in the quest for certainty.

So understood, knowledge of necessity is like knowledge of nonexistence. There is no fountain of youth, and it is a reason for believing that there is no such fountain that none of the many who sought one found one, especially if a consequence of the second law of thermodynamics is that the aging process never reverses. Equally, it is impossible that there be a procedure, using only straightedge and compasses, whereby any angle can be trisected. It is a reason for believing such a procedure impossible that centuries of trying to imagine one failed. It is a better reason if, granted that he fully represented all possible constructions by algebraic structures on real numbers, Galois explained such imaginative failures on the grounds that there is no such procedure.

One can hardly claim to have established Descartes's first premise beyond all doubt. Nonetheless, it does answer to something in us. That may be enough to prompt us to see what issues from applying it to the mind–body problem.[8]

3

More on imagination and modality

Different people might state dualism differently. Our version is the thesis that a person does not depend for his existence on having a body. The relevant sort of dependence is modal. The thesis is thus true if and only if it is possible for a person to exist even if he has no body. So since a person is disembodied if and only if he has no body, our version of dualism is true if and only if it is possible for a person to be disembodied.

Let A be a person. Our argument for our version of dualism begins with the following premise:

(1) What A imagines is possible.

From (1) it follows immediately that if A imagines being disembodied, then it is possible for A to be disembodied; let us call this consequence the immediate consequence of (1). Then, from

(2) A imagines being disembodied,

it is concluded that it is possible for A to be disembodied. Our version of dualism follows from (1) and (2).

We are about to look at another statement of dualism about which are clustered roughly three objections to (1), the first premise of our argument for our version of dualism. In order to treat that statement and the objections justly, we should do some to-ing and fro-ing, so with an eye toward keeping our place, we shall impose a bit more architectonic than is usually desirable.

23

THE STATEMENT AND THE OBJECTIONS

"The claim that it is possible that a given person might become disembodied leads to a dualist conclusion about what
that person is only if combined with some sort of essentialist
claim about persons – one that rules out the possibility that a
purely material being might turn into a being totally without
physical properties." There is implicit in this passage a statement of dualism that invokes ideas we have not explicitly
deployed. The key notion seems to be one of purity, and the
implicit version of dualism might be

(3) People are not purely material,

or

(4) People are purely mental.

One should not take it for granted that one knows exactly
what purity is; we shall return to purity per se below.
    Consider the proposition

(5) Anyone who could be disembodied is not purely mate-
     rial,

and the proposition

(6) Anyone who could be disembodied is purely mental.

Whatever purity might be, it is clear that (3) follows from (5)
and our version of dualism; similarly, (4) follows from (6)
and our version of dualism. The contrapositive of (5) is

(7) Anyone purely material could not be disembodied.

This seems to be the essentialist claim mentioned in the passage, or at least a consequence of such a claim.
    "In the absence of independent grounds for thinking that
there could not be a creature psychologically just like me that
is purely material, one obviously is not entitled to assume
that this is impossible. Such a creature would be able to imag-

ine about itself (or seem to imagine about itself) anything I can imagine (or seem to imagine) about myself. It would not be possible for such a creature to become disembodied; this follows from the essentialist principle. So such a creature cannot establish the possibility of its becoming disembodied by imagining (or seeming to imagine) this happening. But if it cannot, neither can I. Nor is there anything mysterious about the idea that a purely material being might be able to imagine (or seem to imagine) itself becoming completely disembodied, for what it can (seem to) imagine about itself will be governed not by what is true of it but by what it knows (or believes) about itself, and there is no reason to think that a purely material being is going to know (or believe) that it is a purely material being."

In this second passage there is an objection from (7) to (1) and its immediate consequence. Consider the following proposition:

(8) It is possible that there be a purely material person who imagines being disembodied.

From (7) and (8) there is an inference to

(9) It is possible that a person who could not be disembodied imagine being disembodied.

Strictly speaking, this is a non sequitur, for we need the necessitation of (7) to get from (8) to (9); but let us not chop logic. From (9) it follows that

(10) It is not necessarily true that a person who imagines being disembodied could be disembodied.

The objector seems to count (10) against the immediate consequence of (1), and thus against (1) also. Let us call this the first objection.

"The advocate of dualism is caught in an incoherent position. Without an essentialist principle of the relevant sort, he can do nothing with the concession, even if we are prepared

25

to make it, that the imaginability of his becoming disembodied establishes the possibility of this – for without the essentialist principle, no dualist conclusion follows. But if he accepts the principle, he is committed to accepting that there are *a posteriori* necessities and impossibilities – and these are precisely the sort of necessities and impossibilities that cannot be shown not to hold in particular cases by what we can imagine. The case for dualism rests at bottom on an irreparably bad argument."

In this third passage, the objector states a dilemma. The first horn is the claim that his version of dualism does not follow from our version without an essentialist principle like (5) or (7). The idea of the second horn seems to be the following. Assume (7), and recall that A is a particular person. From

(11) A is purely material,

it follows that

(12) A could not be disembodied.

If, moreover, B knew that A could not be disembodied, and knew it by inferring it in this way from (7) and (11), B would know *a posteriori* that A is necessarily embodied. But, we are told, such questions of *a posteriori* necessity cannot be settled by the imagination. So far, we might seem to have an objection to (7), or (5), though it should be noted that we have said nothing about how either might be known. But equally, if B knew that A could be disembodied, and knew it by inferring it from (2) and the immediate consequence of (1), then B would know *a posteriori* that it is possible for A to be disembodied. The objector's distrust of the imagination in questions of *a posteriori* necessity should extend to questions of *a posteriori* possibility. So one would expect him to point the second horn of his dilemma not only at (7), but also at (1) and its immediate consequence. At any rate, let us call this objection the dilemma.

26

"Although imaginability may give support to claims of *de dicto* possibility it cannot in general be used to support claims of *de re* possibility. What I concede is true is that for any pair of phenomenal descriptions that could be descriptions of, respectively, a parcel of matter and a sample of liquid, it is possible *de dicto* that something of the one description should dissolve in something of the second. (Actually even that seems questionable to me.) But plainly it does not follow from this that it is possible *de* any parcel of matter and any sample of liquid that the first could dissolve in the second. And in the case of disembodiment, I can allow that what we can imagine establishes the *de dicto* possibility that there should be someone, psychologically like me, who is capable of becoming disembodied, and still deny that considerations of imaginability establish that it is possible *de* me that I should become disembodied." Let us call this the *de dicto* objection.[1]

ON THE FIRST OBJECTION

Note first that (10) is consistent with (1) and its immediate consequence; for (10) implies only that the immediate consequence of (1) is not necessarily true, which is compatible with its truth. In order to argue to a revision of (10) incompatible with the immediate consequence of (1), one would seem to need to replace "necessarily true" in (10) by "true"; this in turn would seem to require replacing "it is possible that there be" in (8) by "there is." Proposition (8) thus demodalized entails that something purely material has an imagination, an outright materialist claim.

It is no part of our argument that (1) is necessarily true, and understanding this point is important for a correct understanding of (1) and our argument. Premise (1) is a claim not about the essence of possibility, but about one sort of evidence for claims of possibility. When its being true that *p* would be evidence for its being true that *q*, it is not usually necessarily true that if *p*, then *q*; truth of the conditional

27

suffices. It is part of the objectivity of modal truth that it be independent of how we know it; it is part of the objectivity of the possibility that p that it be independent of A's imagining that p. It is a fundamental mistake to think of (1) as a necessary truth.

Premise (1) is a principle of an epistemology of modality, and the leading analogy of that epistemology is that imagination is to knowledge of nonactual possibility as perception is to knowledge of actuality. To be sure, the verb "to see" is sometimes so used that a person cannot truly be said to see that p unless it is in fact true that p, and it may be that the verb "to imagine" is sometimes so used that a person cannot truly be said to have imagined that p unless it is possible that p. But when matters are murky, one may say that it looks to be the case that p, and this may be so even if it is not true that p. The possibility of such a cleavage between visual experience and how things actually are is an aspect of the objectivity of truth; it is also the gap bridged by visual experience as evidence for belief. So if modal truth is also to be objective, we should allow for the possibility that one might seem to oneself to have imagined that p and yet not have; this opens a gap bridged by experiments in the imagination as evidence for modal beliefs. As a disbelief in subjective idealism should make one resist the dictum that to be is to be perceived, so an inclination toward the objectivity of nonactual possibility should make one resist the dictum that to be possible is to be imagined. Nevertheless, as perception is our favored, and perhaps only, basic epistemic access to actuality, so imagination is our favored, and perhaps only, basic epistemic access to nonactual possibility. When one has looked long and hard, when it has always looked to be the case that p, and when one has no good reason to think otherwise, then one has good reason to think that p. Similarly, when one has imagined as inventively as one is able, and it has always seemed clearly to be the case that p in whatever scenario one has spun out, and one has no good reason to think otherwise, then one has good reason to think it is possible that p. In neither case is one guaranteed success: objectivity always leaves open the possibility of error. But in both cases, one has the best of the basic sort of evidence available. In both cases, illusions occur. Optical illusions are familiar. As we have seen, one might think one can imagine going back in time; one visualizes the world as it was when one's father was a boy and thinks one imagines being there too. The hitch comes when one asks what would happen if one killed one's father during his boyhood. No matter what one imagines, there is no guarantee that one has not overlooked some such important hitch; no matter how closely one peers at an object, there is no guarantee that one has not succumbed to some subtle optical illusion. But after a while the absence of evidence for hitches becomes evidence for the absence of hitches; one can only take one's best shot by inferring to the best explanation of what one clearly and persistently seems to see or to imagine, namely, that it is actual or possible.

Second, it is important to be clear about the purport of the first objection. It is not claimed that (8), or even less its demodalized version, is true. Hence, it is not claimed that (10) is true, or that (1) is false. Instead, the objection seems to be about priority in argument. What is said is that in the absence of independent grounds of thinking that (8) is false, one is not entitled to assume that (8) is false. This seems to mean that one is not entitled to (1), or to its immediate consequence, unless one has already shown that (8) is false. The only reason given for requiring this order of argument is the argument from (8) and (7) to (10) and thence to the denials of the immediate consequence of (1) and of (1).

But even supposing that (8) implied the denial of (1), this would not show that one must refute (8) *before* being entitled to (1). For one might just as well refute (8) from (1). Then, of course, it would be circular to argue for (1) from the falsity of (8). So one would want reasons for (1) independent of (8). Since (8) is a claim about mind and matter, it would suffice for independence from (8) to support (1) with reasons having nothing to do with the mind–body problem. This we can do.

Premise (1) figures, as we said, among general principles of an epistemology of modality: (sensuously) imagining that p is good evidence that possibly p; and when it is true that p, and no one with an imagination imagines that not p (despite trying, and because of the nature of the subject matter of the proposition that p, rather than, say, one's having only a limited ability to imagine complexities), then (by inference to the best explanation) this is good evidence that necessarily p. Neither principle says that only the imagination provides evidence for modality. Neither principle says that a single deliverance of the imagination always settles a modal question infallibly. The two principles work together in practice. Suppose we are asked whether necessarily p. We try to imagine that not p, or something sufficient for this. If we succeed, we have evidence that not necessarily p. But if we fail, and if we can explain our failure from the nature of the subject matter of the proposition that p, and if it is true that p, then eventually we have good evidence that necessarily p. Since the principles work together, they are confirmed holistically; support for one confirms the other.

The two principles answer to typical and uncontroversial beliefs about what is, and what is not, possible; and they answer better than linguistic accounts of modal knowledge our century's leading epistemic alternative. Each of us not now at Victoria Station is convinced that he could have been there, and what convinces him seems patently that he can imagine having gone there. It is easy to generate endlessly many uncontroversial examples like this. There are no purple polar bears, but each of us is convinced that there could have been, and what convinces us is that we can visualize a polar bear dyed purple. No leaf is both red all over and green all over at the same time. Each of us is convinced that there could be no such leaf. Pap's dialogue with Putnam showed that this conviction does not spring *ex vi terminorum*.[2] What does so firmly convince us is the blank we draw when we try to visualize a leaf at once red all over and green all over.

This seems as appropriate a place as any to deny that there are different species of possibility. Perhaps all substitution instances of theorems of quantification theory are necessary truths. But talk of logical necessity and possibility should not be confused with a theory of a special sort of modality due somehow to logic; modality is a philosopher's gloss on logic, not part of logic, even modal logic. If one can take possible worlds seriously, and that seems a way of making objective modality vivid, then one can distinguish artificial kinds of possibility like the truths which hold in all worlds that satisfy the natural laws of our world. But equally one could ask which truths persist when telephone numbers are held constant. So far we have been given no reason to interest ourselves in either class. (So-called technological possibility is perhaps as much a type of new actuality as of possibility; for what is technologically possible is usually what has come within the reach of reshuffling or extending recent technique.)

It would be too large a digression to review here the demise of analyticity and semantic accounts of possibility (though it is hard to resist noting that where once upon a time modality was to be explained in terms of meaning, possible-worlds semantics seems to want to explain meaning in terms of modality). What, perhaps strangely, may need saying is that in all philosophically interesting cases, like those of disembodiment or time travel, claims of possibility require support no less than claims of necessity; neither is ever obvious. As theories of meaning grow more baroque, our epistemic access to meaning grows more mysterious, so one should mistrust a claim to possibility grounded in a brute appeal to meaning. Indeed, the order of access seems typically the reverse. For example, when Austin made his famous (if pointless) distinction between the meanings of "accident" and "mistake," he convinced us by showing us how to imagine an accident that is not a mistake, and a mistake that is not an accident.[3] For serious philosophical purposes, hard questions of possibility are all approached in the same way; one experiments in the imagination. It is only misdirection and an excrescence of bad theory to talk here of meaning and semantic consistency; for how does one establish the limits of tolerance of a word's meaning, and how does one learn which sentences are semantically consistent? Insofar as one ever does learn, what one learns seems to be from experiments in the imagination. Assume one knows that the sentence "I am now in Victoria Station" is semantically consistent. Reflecting on recent controversy about the meanings of demonstratives and proper names might make the idea that one has direct epistemic access to the meaning of this sentence perplexing; perhaps one does, but how? But it is easy to imagine oneself being there (and, to anticipate the *de dicto* objection, the burden of proof should fall on anyone who denies that it is oneself whom one is imagining there); imagining being there convinces one that one could be there and thus that the sentence is consistent. There is no such experience as intuiting a meaning; and although one sometimes has strangely firm beliefs about meaning (usually as firm as they are unargued), the fact that they yield to contrary experiments in the imagination indicates that the imagination has the whip hand. Even in the case of bald contradictions of the form p and not p, it is the blank one draws when one tries to imagine that p and not p which sustains the conviction that it could not be true that p and not p, and it is this conviction that elicits a, say, truthtable specification of the "meanings" of the tilde and the ampersand. (There may be a tactical error in defending a nonexclusive reading of the wedge; a student of Quine's more recent relativistic writings[4] might think that there is no fact of the matter about whether exclusivity is to be assigned to the alternatives or to a disjunctive connective.) It seems an honest policy to cut away the curlicues of theory, to refuse to detour through the morass of meaning, to eschew semantics, and to infer from experiments in the imagination to possibility; after all, the philosophical question that first prompted the inquiry was typically one of possibility, not meaning.

There is also something like confirmation of a more theoretical sort. It is an ancient and honorable conviction that all truths of pure mathematics are necessary truths. As Russell saw at about the time of the first edition of *Principia Mathematica*,[5] this conviction does not spring *ex vi terminorum;* for there are existence propositions among the truths of pure mathematics, and as Hume convinced us in Chapter 9 of his *Dialogues Concerning Natural Religion,* no existence proposition is analytic. The ancient and honorable conviction can be explained from Platonism in the metaphysics of pure mathematics and the principles grounding knowledge of modality in the imagination;[6] and this explanation has no rival that does justice to the metaphysics of mathematics. By inference to the best explanation, we thus have further confirmation of the general principles grounding modal knowledge in the sensuous imagination.

There is thus evidence for (1). This evidence is quite independent of the mind–body problem, and thus of (8). So if (1) entails the falsity of (8), we have noncircular evidence against (8). The objector did not claim that (8) is true, nor did he give evidence for its truth. So if we must choose between (1) and the denial of (8), the balance of the evidence favors (1).

If we do test claims of possibility against the imagination, we seem to get a good argument against (9). To make out (9) would seem to require us to imagine a person who is necessarily embodied but imagines being disembodied. This in turn seems to require us to imagine an embodied person whom we are unable to imagine disembodied, though he does. In order for us to imagine him imagining himself disembodied, it would be best and most convincing for us to put ourselves in his shoes and limn for ourselves the imaginings he has of himself disembodied. If we do so, we will thereby have imagined him disembodied, thus frustrating the requirement that we be unable to imagine him disembodied. In the absence of an alternative epistemology for modality, and none has been suggested, (9) seems doubtful. So if (9) follows from (7) and (8), at least one of these is also doubtful.

ON THE DILEMMA

It would seem unsound strategy for us to assume responsibility for the views of Saul Kripke. We, like Kripke on occasion, are following Descartes; and Kripke needs no help from us.[7] But to a certain extent, dealing with the second horn of the dilemma requires us to review some of Kripke's ideas. Consider the proposition that it is essential to this desk that it be made of wood. Kripke thinks this proposition is known *a posteriori*.

The following reasoning is valid:

> If this desk is made of wood, then it is essential to this desk that it be made of wood.
> This desk is made of wood.
> Therefore, it is essential to this desk that it be made of wood.

If the conclusion is known, and known via this reasoning, then it is known *a posteriori* because the second premise is known *a posteriori*. But how is the first premise known? The idea seems to be that nothing could be this very desk unless it were made out of wood; but beyond that, in which "could" is already a modal operator, Kripke says nothing about how we know the first premise. A good reason for believing the first premise would be that one is unable to imagine something's being this very desk unless it is made of wood. Alternatively, if one can imagine this very desk made of something other than wood, then one would and should doubt Kripke's first premise. (On neither alternative is one asked to imagine evidence about the composition of the desk.) We need not decide this example in order to discern that, here, modal belief follows the imagination. Quite singular questions of *a poste-*

34

riori necessity are to be settled partly by the exercise of the imagination.

Kant wrote, "Experience teaches us that a thing is so and so, but not that it cannot be otherwise." If Kripke is right, Kant's claim must be restricted. Still, in the way that there are perceptual experiences of shape, weight, color, texture, and so forth, there are no experiences of necessity or of nonactual possibility. So it is much more than difficult to think how an introduction of necessity, like Kripke's first premise, could be established otherwise than by the imagination.

Consider the example in the *de dicto* objection. The objector seems to think that it is impossible that a lump of gold dissolve in a glass of water, that he knows this *a posteriori,* and that a person suitably ignorant of the chemistries of gold and water could imagine a lump of gold dissolving in a glass of water. Notice that he does not explain how he knows it is impossible for gold to dissolve in water. But it is easy to see how the naïve person's imagination might go. Visualize removing your favorite piece of gold jewelry and setting it on your desk beside a glass of water. (To anticipate, so far there are no grounds for doubting that it is your very own ring, say, that you visualized; and if you are familiar with your ring, it is hard to think what might be wanted by someone who asked how you know it is your own ring that you visualized.) Imagine putting your ring in the glass. As you watch, wisps waiver off your ring in the water, and as time goes on, there is less and less of your ring there. But when you boil the water off, a rind of gold dust is left inside the glass. If the philosopher insists that it cannot have been your gold ring that you imagined dissolving in the water, one should ask him how he knows, for so far he has only insisted.

He might tell you about an actual mechanism of dissolving. In a molecule of H_2O, the two hydrogen atoms are not symmetrically placed about the oxygen atom. So near the molecule, the electrical forces responsible for the valences of the atoms do not exactly cancel. A water molecule is not electrically neutral in its immediate neighborhood, and this pull is strong enough to break the electrical bonds in, say, a crystal of table salt. Presumably he should also tell you something about the bonding chemistry of gold; but why should we do all his work for him? Even so, he has not only to explain the actual chemistry, but more importantly to show that it is necessarily so. The chemistry may be in standard textbooks, but the grounds for his modal claim are conspicuous by their absence. Indeed, so far the only grounds for any modal claim is the experiment in your imagination; and if he did explain the actual chemistry, that would probably provide material for your imagination to vary. Suppose you had looked through Galileo's telescope and seen moons wheeling about Jupiter. How would you have answered the theologians who refused to look and insisted that although it might be (*de dicto*) possible that things like moons revolve about something like Jupiter, the *res* could not be so related? The claim sounds more like *a priori* prejudice than *a posteriori* necessity. So long as no sort of grounds (other than contrary imagination) are provided, modal belief is no more able to resist the imagination than ordinary belief is able to resist vision.

Nowhere is it explained how or why knowledge of Scientific Fact and Law, either all by themselves or in conjunction with some unstated, and thus unargued, philosophical premises, issues in knowledge that gold cannot dissolve in water, and to blame "false" modal belief on scientific ignorance is not to fill in the enthymemes. Indeed, when one is told that gold must have atomic number 79, one might begin to wonder whether this claim entails that gold must have an atomic number and so cannot be continuous stuff, but must be corpuscular. That may, for all one knows, be true, but one would like an explanation of how it is known. The odd thing is that one is not told anything about how the essentialist claim is known. One idea might be that if sodium and chlorine, the actual sodium and chlorine around here, were both continuous stuffs, then they could not be sufficiently different in kind to combine in constant proportions by weight as in table salt. But that claim seems like an invitation to ingenuity; could one imagine how actual sodium and chlorine might be continuous stuffs and yet have a chemistry? Besides, one should not be suckered into accepting an unfair share of the burden of proof; it has yet to be explained how one knows that actual sodium and chlorine could not be continuous stuffs with a chemistry. It is to be hoped that the sequence of modal claims will somewhere touch down in experience, and for claims of necessity and nonactual possibility it is hard to see where touchdown might come if not in the imagination.

Let us take up part of the burden of proof briefly. Perhaps lumps of two sorts of continuous stuffs would have to be knotted to make compounds. The stuffs no more come in natural strands than clay falls into plate-sized blobs for throwing; and any bit, however small, of stuff of one sort can be split into two bits of the same sort of stuff. (Go to your local chemistry department and ask to see samples of sodium and chlorine. Stare at them long enough to fix these samples in your mind. Then of each bit of a single sort that you imagine, imagine it divided into smaller bits of the same kind and that many bits of each kind be so divided in arbitrarily different ways.) The stuffs might be typed by features like density and viscosity connected with, say, the thickness of the strands into which blobs of them may be shaped. If the strands are too short, the knots will not close because the strands are too thick; and if the strands are too long, the dangly bits break off the knots. Thus, density by volume might yield constant enough proportions by weight between the different stuffs in the knots. The kinds of chemical bonds might be kinds of knots. The knots themselves might explain the illusion of natural corpuscles of matter, though the knotted stuffs can be untied and the separate strands lose all identity when mushed into a bigger blob of their same sort of stuff, so the corpuscular appearance really is an illusion. Of course, we will need an agency, in the role of charge, to shape strands and tie knots.

But no (perhaps legendary) Hegel of the necessity of contemporary natural science, the new Absolute realizing itself in Nature (or philosophical opinion), should pretend to know what charge is.

The claim that continuous stuffs could have a chemistry is not utterly unlike the claim that one could be disembodied. In both cases, naïveté seems favorably if tentatively inclined, whereas twentieth-century sophistication may have been trained to resist. So in the case of the mind, a perhaps initially naïve story about what it would be like to be disembodied must be spelled out to a twentieth-century audience; and it is not obvious that a story about what a chemistry of continuous stuffs would be like could not be spelled out even to reaction equations. In both cases, experiments in the imagination are what is wanted; otherwise, there are no data against which to judge opinion. If both stories can be told without a hitch, we then have some evidence for the naïve views; but if either always draws a blank, and especially if that blank is always where something important should go, we have some evidence for the corresponding sophisticated view. As seeing is believing, so modal belief follows the imagination; and in rough country where the imagination has not yet peered, firm modal belief seems a bit presumptuous.

Now let us turn to Kripke's ur-example, *a posteriori* knowledge of necessary identity. As before, the reasoning is valid:

If x is y, then x is necessarily y.
x is y.
Therefore, x is necessarily y.

When the conclusion is known via this reasoning, it is known *a posteriori* in those cases where the second premise is so known. Here, as Ruth Marcus showed, the first premise can be inferred from Leibniz's law and the premise that everything is necessarily self-identical. How is this known? Since the concept of identity is primitive, if any is, it is hard to believe that there is a good argument from a definition of "is

38

identical with" alone to, for each x, the conclusion that x is identical with x. There are, of course, second-order definitions of identity. But since they are not arbitrary stipulations, their adequacy must be demonstrated.[8] This is done by taking instances of the definiens for predicates either with "is identical with" or with a term like "unit set" defined in terms of "is identical with," and in either case reflexivity is merely assumed. If such substituents are forbidden, it is far from clear that the second-order definition is adequate; it is then a version of the identity of indiscernibles, which ought not to be quite so controversial if it is analytic. But there is no need to flounder in the morass of meaning. One draws a blank when one tries to imagine an object not identical with itself, and that is what convinces one that each thing is necessarily self-identical. Pondering *a posteriori* knowledge of necessity confirms the epistemology of modality grounded in the imagination.

Of course, none of this means that any single exercise of the imagination is infallible grounds for modal belief. The leading idea of the epistemology is an analogy: as perception is to knowledge of actuality, so imagination is to knowledge of nonactual possibility. It is part of the analogy that as perceivers can overlook difficulties for what on the basis of perception they believe actual, so imaginers can overlook difficulties for what on the basis of imagination they believe possible (and know by perception to be nonactual). Perhaps what we think we can imagine is governed by what we believe and by our ignorance; the analogous claim about what we think we can perceive has often been urged. But warnings against the pernicious influence of prejudice and ignorance no more cast a particular doubt on a particular claim to nonactual possibility justified by the imagination than they cast a particular doubt on a particular claim to actuality justified by perception. Warnings against prejudice and ignorance should indeed be heeded by dualists, but they should also be heeded by materialists. Materialists in particular must be careful about scientism. At any rate, fallible as we are, we have no good way to introduce necessity or nonactual possibility into *a posteriori* knowledge other than by the imagination.

ON THE *DE DICTO* OBJECTION

Contemporary interest in the medieval distinction between the *de dicto* and the *de re* traces back to Quine[9] and has concentrated on modal and propositional attitude contexts. To illustrate the second case, if one's wife says that she wants there to be a meal on the table when she gets home, she does not usually mean that there is a meal in the oven and she wants it shifted to the table; she wants a meal to be prepared. Here the existential quantifier represented by "there to be" lies in the scope of the verb "want" of propositional attitude. But if she says that there is a man at the party she wants one to meet, the man is already there, and the verb of propositional attitude lies in the scope of the existential quantifier. The first might, a bit fancifully, be said to state her attitude, desire, toward a dictum, that there be a meal on the table when she gets home, and not toward some particular meal that already exists when she speaks; but the second states her attitude toward, in part, a particular man whom she wants one to meet. The first is said to be *de dicto,* and the second, *de re.*

A similar distinction can be made in the case of singular terms like definite descriptions, which, according to Russell's theory of descriptions, represent underlying quantifiers with scopes. If our passenger says that we should stop at the next restaurant, it may be that he knows the route and a particular restaurant coming up next is a good place to stop. Here his remark is *de re,* and the operator represented by "should" might be said to lie in the scope of the quantifier that, Russell taught, underlies "the next restaurant." But it may be that he is only tired of driving and wants to stop soon at a comfortable place. Then his remark is *de dicto,* and the quantifier lies in the scope of the operator.

40

It is more controversial whether the distinction further extends to singular terms, like proper names and demonstratives, where it is less plausible that there is an underlying quantifier. Much of the interest in the distinction has focused on inferential connections between the two forms; David Kaplan dubbed inferences from the *de dicto* form to the *de re* form exportation because the singular term (in that case) is exported from the scope of the verb of propositional attitude.[10] Broadly speaking, there are two schools of thought about when exportation is justified. One view, due to Brian Loar, can be understood as a sophistication of Russell's theory of descriptions; the issue here is how much of the description is exported and how much also remains within the scope of the verb of propositional attitude.[11] The most intriguing element in Kaplan's own view is the thought that a singular term *t* denoting an object *x* may be exported from, to speak loosely, a person A's propositional attitudes only when *t* expresses something like an idea of A's caused in a suitable way by *x*. Kaplan's view thus fits neatly into a program of naturalizing the mind.

The *de dicto* objection reads the sentence "I imagine being disembodied" as "I imagine that I be disembodied." It claims that this propositional attitude can only be *de dicto*, that the second occurrence of "I" cannot be exported, and that it is not oneself whom one imagines being disembodied. Or at least it reads "I could be disembodied" as "It is possible that I be disembodied," claims that the modality is *de dicto*, and denies that it is oneself who could be disembodied.

The pronoun "I" seems more a demonstrative than a proper name or, especially, a definite description. It is not obvious that Russell's theory of descriptions will often apply happily to its occurrences in context, and it is not obvious that it represents anything underlying including an operator, like a quantifier, with a scope to compete with the scopes of "imagine" and "possible." Moreover, if one imagines walking through Trafalgar Square and says that one could have been walking there, the question of how one knows it is oneself whom one is imagining, or who could have been there, seems more than a bit odd. Of course, it is notoriously difficult to articulate an idea of oneself or to explain how one gets and develops one. But that might be because thinking about oneself is almost always more a matter of (unknown) causal relations with oneself than of wielding an inarticulate idea of oneself. If so, the presumption should be that Kaplan-style conditions for exportation and the *de re* are met, so an unsupported burden of proof lies on the objector to show that they are not met in the case of disembodiment.

The *de dicto* objection seems to come to the claims that the objector can imagine a creature who could not be disembodied but who imagines being disembodied and that consequently what the creature imagines could not be true of itself. It will not do just to assert the first claim baldly. That claim should be tested against experiments in the imagination. Moreover, since as Kant saw there is no such thing as an experience, even visualization, of necessity or of nonactual possibility, the content of what is to be tested against experiments in the imagination should have modal expressions like "could not" squeezed out. Then, too, we have uncovered and exhibited a hitch that explains why, appearances perhaps notwithstanding, the objector will fail to make out his first claim; he will draw a blank when he tries to make out both the claims that the creature could not be disembodied and that it imagines being disembodied. The objector may have at the back of his mind general worries about personal identity; we will return to these later. For now, and more specifically, it may be worth remarking that we have been offered nothing better than materialist dogma for being more worried that it is oneself whom one will shortly imagine being disembodied than that it is oneself whom one has imagined walking in Trafalgar Square. What convinces one about the *res* oneself that one could have been walking in Trafalgar Square is imagining of oneself that one be walking there. We have been given no good reason to doubt what seems equally plain, namely, that if we imagine disembodiment of ourselves, then we have good reason to believe disembodiment possible of ourselves. The Latin jargon *de dicto* insulates the claim that one is necessarily embodied against oneself imagined disembodied only through the inert insistence that nothing imagined disembodied could be oneself; nothing in this ploy explains how one might know of oneself that embodiment is necessary.

ON PURITY

Now, finally, let us look at purity, and let us begin by thinking about the ship of Theseus. At any one moment, we know that the ship is there, composed of wooden boards, only by perception; that knowledge of actuality is *a posteriori*. Nonetheless, we believe, the ship is not dependent for its existence on the matter in the boards composing the ship at any one time. For we can imagine the ship persisting though all its boards be replaced, and this convinces us that the ship could exist even if all its matter were replaced. But we cannot imagine the ship persisting though all its boards be destroyed without replacement, and this convinces us that the ship depends for its existence on being, as it were, embodied. We are convinced, by the imagination, that if the ship is embodied, it is essentially embodied.

The objector may understand purity as entirely nonmodal; he may believe that it is for neurophysiological examination alone to settle whether people are purely material. But pondering the natural reasoning in the preceding paragraph makes it convincing that shipwrights and sailors are not much better placed than, say, landlubber philosophers to settle whether the ship of Theseus is purely embodied; on reflection, that reasoning also supports the idea that purity has a modal component. It is perhaps more than merely difficult to articulate the idea of purity cleanly. But on one perhaps more or less intuitive understanding, the ship is purely embodied if and only if it is embodied and, as it were, there is nothing to it outside its embodiments. This last, awkward clause is elusive, but it seems to mean that there is nothing to the ship outside its possible embodiments. Even if it is always in fact composed only of oak, it is not purely oaken if it could have been entirely repaired with boards made of some other wood; for then what it is, its identity, does not depend on its being composed of oaken boards. What is purely oaken, perhaps an oak tree, depends for its existence on being composed of oak; the ship does not, so it is not purely oaken even if in fact it is always composed only of oak. For what it is, its identity, its purity as it were, does not depend on its being composed of oak. The upshot of these reflections is that the ship is purely embodied if it is embodied and there is nothing to it outside its possible embodiments. Put a bit more cleanly, this last clause entails that it could not but be embodied. Conversely, the attempt to articulate what more there is to purity than essence seems to produce only mess. On the only apparent clean rendering, the ship is purely embodied if and only if it is essentially embodied; and at any rate, it is purely embodied only if it is essentially embodied. (Essence is also often implicit in talk of the nature of a thing, so one should not let talk of natures flummox one into conceding an essentialist claim too easily, but rather ask whether the thing must be as it is by nature.)

On this understanding, such as it is, of purity, (5) seems true. It seems that anyone purely material is purely embodied. But even if we are always in fact embodied, we are not purely embodied if we could be disembodied; for then what we are, our identities, do not depend on being embodied. Thus, anyone who could be disembodied is not purely material. This last result is (5), and we have derived it without explicitly mentioning the modal component of purity. With that component explicit, the argument might go as follows. Anyone purely material is essentially material, and thus, so

44

long as he still existed, would be material no matter what might happen to him. If he could be disembodied, he would then have no body, and so not be material. Hence, he could not be disembodied. Thus, anyone purely material could not be disembodied. This last result is (7), which is equivalent to (5).

Proposition (6) also seems true. Anyone who could be disembodied would then have no body; all there would then be to him would be his mind. But what he is, his identity and existence, does depend on his mind. For if his mind were to cease to exist, that would be his annihilation; and even if he is always in fact embodied, were his mind to cease to be, that too would be his death in the sense of annihilation. So anyone who could be disembodied is mental and there is nothing to him outside the possibilities for his mind. Hence, anyone who could be disembodied is purely mental. This last result is (6).

To say of anyone who could be disembodied that even if he is always embodied, were his mind to cease to be, that would be his annihilation may leave a residual question: what happens to his body when his mind ceases to be? Ordinarily, of course, life departs with the mind, and the body falls down and just lies there beginning to rot. But we can imagine that the body continue to move about, exhibiting all its usual behavior including speech; so we have reason to think this possible. But if that were to happen, then one might ask, is he, or are he and his mind, still there in his purely physical remains? No; *ex hypothesi* all his experience, perception, sensation, thought, feeling, belief, imagination, hope, fear, emotion, will, ego, decision, intention, memory, desire, intellect, character, personality, and everything else mental to him are gone.

The thought of this possibility may evoke a certain vertigo. That is because we are imagining something (behavior including speech) without its usual and perhaps only intelligible cause (the mind). But vertigo notwithstanding, the absence of a cause is not impossible; we learned long ago that it is not a necessary truth that every event have a cause. We shall return to this point later, but for now note that we can visualize a rabbit popping into being from nowhere in an otherwise empty universe; so we have reason to think that possible. *Ex hypothesi* there are no prior events in the history of this universe that could be causes of its rabbit episode. Equally, there are no materials from which to devise an explanation of that episode; it is inexplicable as well as uncaused. But it is no more a necessary truth that everything that happens has an explanation than that it has a cause. Similarly, we were just now imagining something (behavior including speech) without its usual and indeed only intelligible cause (the mind).

It is this possibility that raises the epistemic problem of other minds: given that all each of us perceives of other people is the behavior exhibited by their bodies, what justifies us in believing that there are other people, that is, minds responsible for that behavior? It confirms dualism that it explains why this genuine philosophical problem is a problem. A gesture toward an answer is: by inference to the best explanation. Given the behavior, our best and indeed only detailed explanation is, in very broad strokes, to suppose the behavior due to a person whose mind forms, most importantly, beliefs and desires that make his body's behavior action and whose beliefs are frequently produced by perception. That being our best and, insofar as we have worked it out, only detailed explanation, we have reason to believe that there is a mind in there. Note that inference to the best explanation may justify us in believing to exist hypothetical entities that we do not, and perhaps cannot, perceive. All this is epistemological argument for the existence of other minds; metaphysical argument for dualism is argument about the nature of minds.

The objector said that an essentialist thesis of the sort a dualist in his sense needs should rule out the possibility that a purely material being turn into a purely nonmaterial being.

On the present understanding, what is purely material is material and there is nothing to it outside its possible materializations. The awkwardness of this clause is part of the elusiveness of purity, but the clause entails that a purely material thing is essentially material; thus, it could not be nonmaterial and so *a fortiori* could not be essentially nonmaterial; from this, on the present understanding of purity, it follows that it could not be purely nonmaterial.

Now let us return to the first objection. We have set out evidence for (1) that has nothing to do with the mind–body problem and thus does not assume the falsity of (8). This includes not only the evidence between the sixth and ninth paragraphs of the section entitled "On the first objection," but also that in the first three paragraphs of "On the dilemma" and that in the first paragraph of the present section. Although there was a fallacious argument purportedly from (8) to the denial of (1), no evidence for (8) has been offered, so even if that argument were valid, there is no evidential support for it to transmit to the denial of (1). In the last paragraphs of "On the first objection," we saw a good argument from (1) against (9), so we have evidence against (9). Thus, if (9) follows from (7) and (8), then since we have established (7), we have evidence against (8). [Indeed, since purity has a modal component, our argument from (1) against (9) was already an argument against (8).] None of this reasoning begs any question or gets backward any order of argument that may be legitimately required. We have argued that dualism can be established from the imaginative epistemology of modality and what we imagine. Since dualism is and ought to be incompatible with materialism, it is to agree with us to claim that, given that we imagine being disembodied, materialism is incompatible with the imaginative epistemology of modality; the contrapositive of a result, and what is equivalent to the contrapositive, are not an objection to that result. If our position were "incoherent," so would be any "objection" equivalent to that position; if an argument from A to the denial of B were "irreparably bad," so would be the reverse argument from B to the denial of A.

To assert (8) without evidence would come to denying (1) without evidence, and to deny (1) would threaten all serious claim to modal knowledge. Since, as Quine has long urged, we really must chose between materialism and modality, it seems only fair to allow both sides a hearing, especially since materialism is now orthodox among philosophers of mind. Moreover, if one cannot consistently believe both, in the ordinary way, that though one is not at Victoria, one could have been and, for elaborate philosophical reasons, that one is purely material, then since the first is more evident to common sense than the second, someone like Moore might well think it irrational to deny the first on the basis of the second. At any rate, materialists should warn us that we must give up claims to nonactual possibility in order to agree with them. One who thinks we are purely, and so essentially, material, but admits that some of us imagine being disembodied, has to deny (1); he thus denies us ordinary epistemic access to nonactual possibility. That is too large a price to pay, or at least too large to pay blithely. The materialist who takes nonactual possibility seriously owes us an alternative epistemology for modality, and there is no reason to believe that there is one that both is generally acceptable and does not refute materialism.

Now let us return to the second horn of the dilemma. Assume that B knows (7), that B knows of A that A is purely material, and that B concludes, and so comes to know, of A that A could not be disembodied. On the present understanding, purity has a modal component. So if B's knowledge of A that A is purely material conforms to Kripke's pattern, B reasoned from

(13) If A is material, then A is purely material,

and

(14) A is material,

48

to conclude of A that A is purely material. Then B's knowledge of A that A could not be disembodied will be *a posteriori* if his knowledge of A that he is material is *a posteriori;* and one expects that B would know of A that A is material by experience. But the modality in B's *a posteriori* knowledge of A that A could not be disembodied is first introduced, on Kripke's pattern, by (13); purity has a modal component. Fallible though we are, we have no good way to introduce modality into *a posteriori* knowledge other than by the imagination. So B's *a posteriori* knowledge of A that A could not be disembodied is justified partly by the exercise of B's imagination.

Something very like B's knowledge is exhibited in our knowledge of the ship of Theseus. Our knowledge that it is in fact embodied and composed of oak is *a posteriori,* and the shipwright's superior experience may give him authority about whether it is actually oak of which it is composed; this is like B's knowledge of (14). Then we ask whether, given that it is composed of oak, it is essentially composed of oak; so we try to imagine it made of something else. The shipwright's superior experience may highlight for him difficulties landlubbers overlook in how they think they imagine that very ship composed of some wood other than oak. On the other hand, occultation by the conventional wisdom sometimes blinkers an expert's imagination of other possibilities. But the exercise is still an exercise of the imagination; that is our only basic epistemic access to nonactual possibility. It is our inability, in which the shipwright is unlikely to be more adept than the rest of us, to imagine that very ship disembodied that convinces us that it is essentially embodied; and once we are so convinced, we are as far as we are likely to get toward knowing that it is purely embodied. Superior knowledge, of course, has its proper part in imaginative investigations of nonactual possibility and of necessity; but that fact does not make those investigations nonimaginative.

4

The senses, part I

The second premise of Descartes's argument was the claim that you can imagine being disembodied. To be convinced of that claim, you should require a story, a recipe the successful execution of which will enable you to imagine being disembodied. Here we begin such a story.

But first, enter the prologue. How much of you is it reasonable to expect might persist through disembodiment? You now have, one presumes, a body. It is clearly not reasonable to expect a recipe for imagining that you have a body when you have no body. Similarly, because a disembodied person should be immaterial, you will not have a leg to stand on, nor a pancreas, nor lips or a smile, nor hands or a fist. It is you in your mental dimensions that should persist through disembodiment. You have, as it were, three mental dimensions. First, there are those faculties that are conduits from the material world into your mind. The only sure examples of these are the five senses: sight, hearing, smell, taste, and touch. Some include the sensations, like pain and itches, among the senses; and though we will not class the sensations exactly with the five senses, we will discuss them with the sense of touch. Second, there are the intrapsychic functions, the so-called higher faculties. These include most of the so-called propositional attitudes specified by a verb ("believes," "desires," "thinks," "wonders," "dreams," and so on) followed usually by "that" (though "wonders" takes "whether") followed by a sentence. (To use this jargon, you do not have to believe that to wonder is to take an attitude toward a proposition; the term of art, propositional attitudes, has a grammati-

50

cal rather than psychological source.) The emotions should probably be classed as intrapsychic as well. Third, there are the conduits from the mind to the world of which the central examples are actions, like moving yourself around the world (locomotion), rearranging your organization (change of attitude), and manipulating objects that (usually) lie outside your body.

Descartes is sometimes faulted for concentrating too much on the second of these three classes, and on the intellectual propositional attitudes in particular. (Indeed, he may have restricted the mind, that is, you, to the second dimension.) We shall concentrate much more on the first and third and say less about the disembodiment of the second; the difference in *Gestalt* between our dualism and Descartes's arises from this source.

This is not meant to suggest that any of these faculties are essential or necessary to being you or to being a person with a mind. There have been blind people and paralyzed people. Indeed, one might at least play with the idea that a person could continue to exist even if he lost all his mental faculties. But it is no part of our purpose to argue for so extreme a thesis here. The point is rather that dualism would not be refuted just because some one of all these many faculties could not be imagined to persist through disembodiment. On the other hand, the interest, and perhaps the content, of dualism varies directly with the number and variety of faculties that can be imagined to survive loss of the body. It therefore behooves us to save as much as we can.

Let us begin the story with the senses, and with sight in particular. In order to tell a convincing story about sight, we are required to do two things at once; we must know both what sight is and that, whatever it is, you can imagine yourself to have it even if you were disembodied. As for what sight is, it is a necessary condition of sight that one have visual experience. Sense-datum philosophy having been so long in bad odor, what needs arguing on this point is that

51

there is such a thing as visual experience. But it seems evident that three phenomena – sight, visualizing (in the mind's eye), and, at least almost always, dreaming – have something in common. This commonality is visual experience; so there is visual experience. Visualizing (as in hallucinating) a dagger is enough like seeing one for Macbeth not to be sure which is his state; and dreams seem always to involve visual experience that (Malcolm notwithstanding)[1] can make us think we have seen monsters. Austin notwithstanding,[2] it seems clear that visualizing, seeing, and dreaming do have something in common, namely, visual experience. (Nothing in this argument requires visual experience to play the epistemic role in which sense data were once cast, so we are not committed to the existence of sense data. Moreover, precisely because visual experience is common to three phenomena only one of which is right, having visual experience is not sufficient for sight. But note that since those who no longer have eyes can visualize, it is possible to have visual experience at a time when one has no eyes.)

Suppose that one morning, still embodied, you awaken. Before raising your eyelids, you grope your way over to your mirror. Facing it, you raise your lids; you can see in the mirror that your eye sockets are empty, that your eyeballs are missing; the point is that you can visualize your face with empty eye sockets as it would look to you in the mirror. This is, of course, curious. So raising your hand, you probe an empty eye socket with one of your little fingers. You can visualize how that little finger probing the socket would look; and you can do for touch as visualizing is to sight what that finger might feel like against the flesh of your empty eye socket. Growing more curious, you saw round the top of your head, peel back the top of your skull, and peer into your brain pan; it, too, is empty, and again the point is that you can visualize how your empty brain pan would look to you in the mirror. (In an alternative version of this story, you might imagine that the region of the confluence of your lines of sight gradually slips down your cheeks, over your jaw line and down your neck, and thence down to flank your navel, and that then, from there, you watch your eyes wither and their fragments blow away in the wind.)

But now we have a recipe for the visual experience you would have of yourself without eyes or a brain. These are most people's favored candidates for bodily organs essential to sight. You do not need your hands, feet, or pancreas to see, so imagine them away; indeed, for any one of your remaining organs, you can imagine visual experience of yourself without it. Moreover, you can visualize what you would see in the mirror even if all of the rest of your body were gone. To be sure, you see none of your body, since that is gone now; but you see (i.e., have a visual experience of), from a certain point of view, the reflection in the mirror of the room behind you. So you have a recipe for visual experience of yourself disembodied.

There are at least two immediately pressing questions about the story so far. The first is about location. Embodied people are (at least typically) located in space where their bodies are. But since a disembodied person has no body, where is he? Any person, even disembodied, who exists in this world must be somewhere. We can only begin to answer this question here. Every visual experience of a scene is an experience of that scene as it would be seen from a certain point of view. We see the various characters in a scene along what we call lines of sight. These lines of sight converge at a point, or at least in a small region, of space. At least part of the disembodied person is at this point or in that region of space, even though it is now no longer occupied, as it once was, by his eyes. (There will be more to location than the region of convergence.)

This makes sense only if the scene, visual experience of which we are imagining, is real. Here we come up against the second immediate question about our story: since visual experience is not by itself sufficient for sight, what more does a

53

disembodied person need in order to see? According to the tradition, sight is distinguished from dreaming and visualizing by veridicality. Veridicality is to experience as truth is to thoughts (propositions, sentences, or statements). As a thought is true precisely in case the world is as one with the thought thinks it to be, so a visual experience is veridical precisely in case the world is as it looks to one with the visual experience. Note that in order for an experience to be veridical, there need be no substantial connection and no transmission or linkage between the experience and that chunk of the world in virtue of which it is veridical. Veridicality requires only, as it were, a coincidence of content between experience and the world. Hence, there is no obstacle at all in the way of supposing that a disembodied person's visual experience be (as it were, barely) veridical, that is, that the world be as it looks to the disembodied person. That understood, we may suppose that the scene of which he has visual experience is real, that therefore his lines of sight coincide with real lines in genuine space, and that consequently the region of convergence of those lines determines a real place in space for part of him to occupy.

But there is more to sight than veridical visual experience, as H. P. Grice showed.[3] Suppose that an embodied man, seated in a darkened room, is having visual experience as of a lighted candle a foot tall a few feet in front of him. Suppose further that there is a lighted candle a foot tall a few feet in front of him. He thus has a visual experience and it is veridical. But now suppose two further things. First, because there is an opaque object between him and the candle in front of him, no light reaches him from that candle. Then why does he have his visual experience? Because, second, some way away, there is a lighted candle a foot tall, the light from which is transmitted to him along an ingenious sequence of mirrors, the last of which is the opaque object before him. Suppose a gun were put to your head and you had to pick one of the two candles and say of it that it is the candle he is seeing. Of the people to whom this choice has been put, all have selected the distant candle whose transmitted light causes his visual experience. Thus, putting the pieces together, we might say that veridical visual experience is sight only if it is caused by that in virtue of which it is veridical. (More than the bare coincidence required by veridicality is necessary for sight.)

Here, for the first time, though in an unusual form, we encounter the problem of causal interaction between matter and disembodied (or disembodiable) minds; it is unusual, perhaps, because the relevant bit of matter is not the person's body, but the objects causally responsible for his veridical visual experience. The first thing to notice, and it is important, is that this is as much a problem about the nature of causation as it is a problem about the nature of mind (or matter). Suppose, for example, we follow Hume in taking constant conjunction to be the core of causation; the idea is that one event is the cause of another precisely in case all events of "the" same kind as the first are followed by events of "the" same kind as the second. It was consciously and avowedly Hume's intention that causation require no occult powers, that is, that given spatial contiguity and temporal priority, causation require no more than bare conjunction, juxtaposition, between tokens of event types. But (once mental events are located in space) there is no more obstacle in the way of supposing a bare constant conjunction between certain mental and certain physical events than between any two types (like different physical types) of events. So on Hume's view of causation, there is no problem whatsoever about supposing that veridical visual experience in the disembodied be caused by that in virtue of which it is veridical. It calls for judgment, but this result hardly seems a solution to the problem of causal interaction between Cartesian minds and matter; instead, precisely because it makes trivial a difficult problem, it is evidence against Hume's view of causation. Hence, since most subsequent philosophical discussions of causation have been footnotes to Hume, we shall need an account of causation before we can return to sight.

But before considering such an account, let us remark that not just any old causation of veridical visual experience by that in virtue of which it is veridical is sufficient for sight. Suppose that (embodied) Ralph is captured by the mad scientist, blindfolded, and injected with chemical C. Chemical C affects Ralph's mind in only one way: it causes in him a visual experience from the right point of view of the mad scientist injecting him with chemical C. (We could suppose this for a vast range of chemicals and, though it is more delicate, with a sensitivity to varying relative separations between Ralph and the scientist. A sound signal or chemical feed from the scientist as he moves about might so alter the position, say, of a radical in the molecules of chemical C as to adjust veridically the visual experience that it causes in Ralph.) Here we have veridical visual experience caused by that in virtue of which it is veridical, but in most people's judgment we do not have sight; Ralph does not, they say, see the scientist inject him with chemical C.

This is sometimes called a problem of appropriate causation because the causation of the veridical visual experience is not appropriate for sight. Problems of appropriate causation seem to infect attempts to analyze a range of mental faculties (like knowledge, *de re* belief, action, and perhaps speaker's reference) in causal terms. These may in turn be regarded as attempts to naturalize the mind, that is, to fit it into the causal nexus that constitutes nature, as opposed to a sort of Kantian tradition that regards the mind as outside nature reflecting it, perhaps as artificially or conventionally (as opposed to naturally or causally) as language describes things. Suppose that Fred were utterly causally isolated from the rest of the world, that you could parse the grammar of Fred's thoughts, and that there were one assignment of objects as denotations of his singular terms and values of his variables and of sets or properties as extensions of his predicates that maximized truth among Fred's beliefs. The tradition we are calling Kantian would be happy to conclude that you had understood Fred's thought correctly. To the extent that you are not happy with this conclusion you will sympathize with attempts to naturalize the mind and thus should take problems of appropriate causation seriously.

However it may be with other faculties, perhaps sight can avoid problems of appropriate causation by requiring that its external causation be carried by the proper medium, namely, light. Suppose that when Ralph is captured and blindfolded by the mad scientist, no unusual chemicals are injected (or otherwise applied) but that the scientist tinkers so that when Ralph's navel is exposed to well-lighted scenes, Ralph is caused (for which we have evidence in that light reflected from the scene traveling in straight rays to Ralph's navel is less energetic after being reflected from his navel than is light reflected from his back) to have visual experiences veridical of those scenes. To be sure, the causation here is unusual, but perhaps it is unusual causation of what is nonetheless sight; we have discovered, as it were, that Ralph's navel has been converted to an organ of vision. (It might help if Ralph's depth perception were impaired but that of people with two navels were not.) If so, we might say that sight is veridical visual experience caused via light by that in virtue of which it is veridical. (When the sun behind you illuminates a stone before you, you see the stone, not the sun, though the light comes originally from the sun. To handle this point, we might say that one sees those objects from which light reaches one along straight or untangled rays; but some bending, as in a mirage or a mirror, may be acceptable, so long as between-ness relations among rays are not too jumbled for questions of veridicality to be settled.)

Grice originally thought that the nature of appropriate causation should be left to the special sciences and that it was enough for the philosopher to get the idea across by pointing to examples. It would be fortunate if the philosopher could do more. Sometimes a worry is expressed that if too much special natural science is built into an analysis of sight, it will turn out that Cicero, to whom such science was not available, had no idea of what sight is. To be sure, if vibrations in the electromagnetic field had to be mentioned by name in the definition of "video," Cicero would not have understood that Latin verb, which seems implausible. But surely Cicero knew that we do not see well in the dark and that we see by means of light; this last is part of the nature of sight (and it does not matter whether it is part of the definition of "video"). (A more delicate judgment is required if straight light rays are part of the nature of sight; but Cicero presumably knew also that we do not see around corners except by means of polished surfaces.)

Even if invoking the medium solves problems of appropriate causation for perception (where the media, like light and sound, are common knowledge), it is not obvious that similar conditions would solve the parallel problems of appropriate causation for other faculties, like *de re* belief or action, where no carrier is commonly known; but then, neither need all such problems have a uniform solution. Then, too, the depth of our account of sight is no greater than its assumption that we can tell which experience is *visual* (rather than, say, auditory). But even so, our recipe for imagining disembodied sight needs an account of causation.

5

Causation

The problem of causal interaction between mind and matter is as much a problem about causation as it is a problem about mind or matter. Regularity theories of causation, however larded over with subjunctives, trivialize the problem; there is no more difficulty about brute constant conjunction between mental and physical events than between some physical events and others. So since the problem of causal interaction between mind and matter is not trivial, we want an understanding of causation that will articulate the severity of that problem adequately.

One might organize one's thinking about causation into a rational reconstruction (and thus, probably, a mythology) of the history of some discussions of the problem. There were people who thought a cause necessitates its effects no less than a conjunction necessitates its conjuncts; Spinoza is the leading example. Hume set himself to argue that causes do not necessitate their effects; we can, perhaps, recover three arguments to this end from his text. The first is an appeal to imagination. Suppose the white ball strikes the black from a certain angle at a certain speed; the black moves off as Newton's laws more or less predict. But we can imagine that both stop dead, or explode, or turn into avocados. Hence, the cause does not necessitate the effect Newton's laws predict, as a matter of fact, correctly. This, it might be thought, is a strong argument for a weak result, namely, that causation is not necessitation as strong as the necessity with which nothing can be red all over and green all over at once; but it allows that there might be in causation a degree of necessity stronger than flabby contingency but short of iron necessity. (But it would need separate argument that such a degree of necessity is significantly large.)

Whereas the first argument is very simple, the second is very theoretical. It depends, first, on an atomic empiricism. Not only do the propositions (or larger units) we believe have to be justified from experience, but also our concepts (which are to beliefs as particles are to atoms) must be derived from experience; all ideas are, in particular, faint copies of experiences. It depends, second, on an atomic theory of meaning; the meaning of a word is an idea expressed by anyone who uses the word meaningfully. It depends, third, on an observation. As Kant put it, experience teaches us that a thing is so-and-so, but not that it cannot be otherwise; in the sense in which there is an experience of yellow and an experience of sweetness, there is no such thing as an experience of necessity. It follows that there is no idea of necessity (save by what seems confused reflection on the succession of our ideas) and thus that "necessitate" is meaningless (save in the same barely conjunctive way). This argument is no better than its two atomic theories, both of which have suffered two centuries of reverses.

But we may be able to excogitate a third argument from his text. First, our principal repository of causal knowledge is natural science. Second, the causal knowledge stored in natural science is *a posteriori,* that is, justified by experience. But third, as in the last argument, there is no experience of necessity. It follows that causation is not necessitation. For if it were, then since the causal knowledge stored in natural science is *a posteriori,* we would have *a posteriori* knowledge of necessitation, and that cannot be since there is no experience of necessitation. This argument is attractive. It has three very plausible premises. Moreover, because it has the consequence that causal knowledge is *a posteriori,* it imposes on accounts of causation the material adequacy condition that empirical evidence for or against causal propositions (or laws) must at least be possible. Hume's version of the regularity theory of causation is conformable to this condition; for temporal priority, spatial contiguity, and constant conjunction are all observable (and perhaps all that is relevant to causation and observable, observability being crucial for Hume, who believed that there are no occult powers). No account of causation is acceptable unless it is compatible with *a posteriori* knowledge of causation; and a good account of causation should fit smoothly into a good account of justification of causal beliefs by experience. So no account of causation in terms of modality that omits an epistemology of modality is to be trusted blindly. (Nelson Goodman makes this point very forcefully.)[1]

Temporal priority and spatial contiguity are connected nowadays with problems in the philosophy of physics, namely, the causal theory of time and action at a distance. It has long been clear that constant conjunction is not sufficient for causation. There are, it seems, two sorts of counterexamples. One sort is due to Nelson Goodman. If all the coins in one's pocket are made of silver, there is a constant conjunction between being a coin in one's pocket and being made of silver. But being in one's pocket does not cause a coin to be made of silver; try to transmute a penny into silver by putting it in a pocket containing only silver dollars. Goodman notes that the present regularity does not sustain, as he puts it, the subjunctive conditional that if this penny were in one's pocket, it would be made of silver. But causal, as opposed to accidental, regularities do sustain subjunctive conditionals.[2] So some have thought that Hume's account somehow supplemented by the subjunctive is sufficient for causation. It is natural to construe a subjunctive conditional as meaning that although its antecedent is not true, it could be, and were this possibility actual, its consequent would be true. If such conditionals are about unactualized possibilities, an account of causation that uses the subjunctive mood requires an epistemology of modality; since empiricism is the only theory of knowledge, or since causal knowledge is *a posteriori,* this epistemology must be empiricist. A counterexample of the second sort is given by the fact that whenever the barometer's needle falls (thusly), it rains; but the falling needle does not cause it to rain. Here, the first event is constantly conjoined with the second and is a good sign of it, but does not cause it; rather, both are effects of some underlying cause (increased relative humidity decreases air pressure to drop the needle and, at the right temperature, condenses out rain drops). The phrase, being joint effects of a common cause, worked into Hume's account (without extensive modification) would make it viciously circular.

There is another and very different tradition of thinking about causation. Among the schoolmen it was a maxim (appealed to by Descartes) that there must be as much reality, neither more nor less, in the cause as in its effect. Contemporary students are sometimes taught to ridicule this maxim on the grounds that the adjective "real" has neither comparative nor superlative; existing or being real is not a stuff of which there can be more and less. Granted; but suppose that they meant "verus," or whatever word they used, as we might use a free variable. Its value, unknown to them, was some quantity or other that is strictly conserved, that is, neither comes into being nor vanishes. This quantity should be located at places and times, and capable of change of place with time, that is, motion. So when an intuitively (that is, naïvely) specified causal chain of events (like the standard billiard table examples) is genuine, the total of this quantity should be conserved along the chain and traceable along its path through space and time; tracing the quantity's motion along the chain would be a way to explain the events in it.

Perhaps the best way to put this idea is to say that in order that thoroughgoing causal explanation be possible, some localizable and conserved quantity should be traceable along causal chains. It is not necessarily true or known *a priori* that nature can ultimately be understood. Once one gives up the idea that nature, having been made by a Mind like ours, must be intelligible, one admits that for all we know we will never understand the basis of nature; Feynman sometimes seems to suggest that such is the message of quantum mechanics.[3] Nor is it necessary that something be conserved. You can picture a world in which from all eternity there was nothing (the vast, dark, empty reaches), into which a rabbit pops into being out of nothing, flails about for five minutes, and then vanishes into nothing, the vast, still dark continuing through all the rest of eternity. In such a world, no physical quantity would be conserved. But equally, because nothing is conserved this world provides no materials from which to fabricate an explanation of its rabbit episode; the presuppositions of the questions "Where did the rabbit come from and how?" and "Where did the rabbit go and what happened to it?" fail. Hence, it may be something we know *a priori* that if thoroughgoing explanation is to be possible, some quantity or other must be conserved; that claim could be taken as a reworking of the schoolmen's maxim.

It seems likely that for centuries, people looked for a conserved quantity traceable along intuitively identified causal chains but that it was not until the last century that nature cooperated by revealing energy (or later, mass–energy) to them. The history here is very complex,[4] but it is not as if Helmholtz said one day, "Look! there is $\frac{1}{2}mv^2$ conserved and traceable along mechanical causal chains." In the seventeenth century, Newton had worked out concepts of velocity (at an instant) and mass (as opposed to weight). It then took a long time to establish that there is a function of these quantities conserved through mechanical processes and convertible at a fixed rate to a quantity conserved through thermodynamic processes, to another quantity conserved through chemical processes, and so on across all known sorts of process. That is how one might picture the origin of the concept of energy. Energy was not first detected and then discovered to be conserved; rather, no detected quantity would have been identified as energy unless there were good reason to believe it conserved.

Since conservation principles are quantitative, energy can be conserved only if it is a quantity. Two confusions need here to be forestalled. First, a quantity is not always a stuff. Water is a stuff. If two rivers, a and b, join in a single stream, c, which later in its delta divides into two streams, d and e, then there is presumably a fact of the matter about how much of the water in d came from a and how much from b. But suppose that two bodies, x and y, collide simultaneously with a third, z, and that as a result, z moves off until it collides simultaneously with u and v, setting them in motion. It would seem that there is no fact of the matter about how much of the kinetic energy of u came from x and how much from y. If so, energy, though it is a quantity, is not a stuff. Second, one should distinguish between quantities and measures. Quantities are objective, out there, independent of us; but measures are our means of detecting quantities. Metaphysics treats quantities; epistemology treats measures. There is no more guarantee that every quantity should be capable of measurement than that all truths should be knowable. Both these points are negative; we shall later look at one positive account of quantity.

We should distinguish between two sorts of conservation principles: global and local. A quantity is globally conserved if and only if the total amount of it at any one time is the same as the total at any other time. In order that a quantity be locally conserved, it must have spatial, as well as temporal, location. Then the quantity is locally conserved if and only if the total amount of it in any volume varies directly with the net amount of it passing into the volume through the surface. Global conservation does not entail local; for if amounts of a quantity that vanish into nothing at one place are always exactly balanced by an equal amount popping into being at another place, then the quantity will be globally but not locally conserved. But suppose a located quantity is not globally conserved; then at some time, an extra amount of it will come into being from nothing or pass away. Let us concentrate on the first alternative. Consider any volume containing the place at which the extra amount of the quantity came into being. In this volume, the amount of the quantity increased, although none of the quantity entered the volume through its surface. Hence, a locally conserved quantity is globally conserved; local conservation is stronger than global. If there were action at a distance, it would violate local conservation, but (though it might require magic) it would not necessarily violate global conservation.

There arises out of the local conservation of energy the idea of the flow of energy; critics of action at a distance typically insist upon flow. Granted that energy (usually) flows along intuitively identified causal chains, there arises the idea of causation as energy flow. Quine is to be honored for many things, not the least of these being that he takes this idea of causation seriously.[5] Following him, think of (physical) events as the material and energic contents of regions of space-time. Assuming local conservation of energy, amounts of energy in an event must have world lines extending backward in time. Quine suggests that any earlier event through which all these world lines pass is a cause of the given event.

This view has certain advantages. First, it shows why a falling barometer needle does not cause rain, and it does so rather more naturally than any regularity theory of causation (like Hume's), even one larded over with the subjunctive mood: no energy emitted by the moving needle becomes energy expended in rainfall (and if it did, the needle's motion would be a partial cause of the rain); instead, the energy expended both in the needle's motion and in the rain presumably flows from prior atmospheric events. The energy flow view provides a very natural way to say all this without using the word "cause." Second, this view turns questions of closed causal loops and reflexivity of causation into interesting, substantial, and properly difficult questions rather than legislates trivial answers to them by building temporal priority into the very definition of causation. How do we know that the world line of an amount of energy might not be a closed curve in space-time? Such a closed curve could easily violate even global conservation; but it would take us too far afield to discuss the matter here.[6]

Third, the view can be used to explain why lawlike regularities sustain subjunctive conditionals but accidental regularities do not. Let us say that a (causal) mechanism is a *pattern* of energy flow. Quine invites us to parse subjunctive conditionals as existentially quantified sentences asserting the existence of (typically unknown) causal mechanisms.[7] Usually the flow will be from events described by the antecedent to events described by the consequent; but it will not be if they describe joint effects of a common cause. When a lawlike regularity picks out a pattern of energy flow connecting two sorts of events, it will entail a subjunctive conditional simply by existential generalization; and since presumably regularities are accidental when there is no pattern of energy flow connecting the sorts of events they constantly conjoin, they will not entail subjunctive conditionals. Fourth, the view meets Hume's adequacy condition on accounts of causation. Though we cannot see amounts of energy in the way we can see amounts of water (perhaps because although both are quantities, water is a stuff, but energy is not), we can sometimes measure amounts of energy and trace patterns of its flow, albeit often indirectly and via theory. Fifth, if the flow of energy really is incompatible with its quantum mechanical discontinuities, then, as Quine points out, the view justifies the belief that quantum mechanics is incompatible with causality (at least in the very small).

Sixth, and most important for present purposes, the view makes properly difficult the problem of causal interaction between matter and disembodied minds. Constant conjunction trivialized that problem. Since it set its face against occult powers, that is, against invisible links or the flow of unper-

66

ceived quantities from cause to effect, it avowedly and intentionally required only brute conjunction for causation; and bare, brute succession between contiguous or coincident mental and physical events is easily imagined. But on the energy flow view, the problem becomes: how could energy of some sort flow between matter and disembodied minds? That question seems adequately perplexing.

But problems also obstruct the view. Suppose a climber shouts abruptly, starting the brooding snowfield into avalanche. Only the tiniest fragment of the energy of the avalanche comes from the climber; most was stored as weight in the high snows. But *the* cause, we say, was the shout. Here it seems right to ride roughshod over common sense; the shout was only a tiny bit of the cause, most of which was the weight of the high snow. But this much of a concession to common sense is possible: suppose that most of the energy in an event enters it along world lines more or less parallel to the (convenient) time axis, but a bit enters along lines more oblique. We could say that to the extent that the world line of a bit of an event's energy is oblique to the world lines of the rest (and those, parallel to the time axis), then to that extent that bit of energy is a moving cause of the event; what common sense thinks is the cause of the avalanche good sense thinks is to a considerable extent a moving cause.

Consider next a refrigerator. The motor makes water in the freeze box turn to ice; as it were, causation goes from the motor to the freeze box. But heat, that is, energy, goes from the freeze box to the motor. So, it might seem, causation moves in a direction opposite to that of energy. Here, perhaps, common sense is confused. First, we must not think of cold as a sort of negative of heat pumped from the motor to the freeze box. For since heat in a gas is the mean kinetic energy of its molecules, if cold were genuinely its negative, then since an amount "plus" its negative makes nought, energy could be destroyed, and that would violate its conservation. (Of course, this is not to deny that when a hot body touches a cold body, they tend to come to the same temperature; heat flows from the hot body to the cold one.) Second, how does a refrigerator work? There runs through it a tube filled with fluid. The motor compresses the fluid into a liquid where the tube is narrow and then pumps it up to the freeze box. There the tube is wider, reducing pressure, and the fluid (which has a low boiling point) boils. Its molecules require energy to leave the liquid and join the boiled-off gas. This energy they take from the water in the freeze box, and when they have taken enough, the attractive (electrical) forces among the water molecules are able to regiment them into crystalline solids, that is, ice cubes. Since heat flows from hotter bodies to cooler ones, the liquid under low pressure is cooler than the water in the freeze box. The gas returns to the motor, where it is again compressed into a liquid, the heat thus extracted being dissipated into the air. A refrigerator is thus a heat-extraction pump, and no matter what common sense thinks, its causation works around the described spatial loop (which is a corkscrew in space-time). The only slightly delicate point emerges more clearly from another example: if we cut off the sunlight from a plant long enough, the plant will die; so the obstructing screen (we say) causes the plant to die, though no energy flows from the screen to the plant. It seems clear what to say here: when a cause, light from the sun, sustains an effect, the life of the plant, by transmitting energy to it, closing down the cause will close down the effect and thus in a derivative sense cause the effect to cease. So in the refrigerator, the motor closes down an effect of heat (gaseousness), which the water reestablishes by freezing; when energy flowing from a cause to an effect is blocked, the effect ends, and in a derivative sense we may say that blocking the flow causes the end of the effect. So the energy flow view of causation can accommodate cases like the refrigerator.

Causation is energy flow, and it is a good reason for believing this thesis that it makes properly difficult the problem of imagining how disembodied people might see.

6

Quantity

Sight, we said, requires veridical visual experience caused by that in virtue of which it is veridical. Causation is the flow of energy, a thesis founded on the local conservation of energy, which is a quantitative principle. Hence, disembodied people could see only if a quantity flows from what they see to them. It is this last requirement, that there be some quantity intrinsic to a disembodied person, that is striking. Are there any really psychological quantities?

One way to approach this question would be to give a general account of quantity and then argue that some mental phenomena determine quantities of that sort. Thus, we ask, what is a quantity?

Mathematical habit makes it natural to think of a quantity q had by objects in a nonempty set A as a function that assigns to each object in A a member of the set R of real numbers. We are interested in relationships between properties of q and structures on members of A; the study of quantities is a branch of applied algebra. For example, q induces a relation NL on A thus: for x and y in A, x is not less in q than y if and only if (iff, for short) $q(x) \geq q(y)$. This relation is obviously transitive,

1. $(xNLy \ \& \ yNLz) \rightarrow xNLz,$

and connected,

2. $xNLy \ \lor \ yNLx$

(which entails reflexivity). Is the converse true? That is, given a transitive and connected relation NL on A, is there a quantity q representing NL in the sense that $xNLy$ iff $q(x) \geq q(y)$? And if so, how much freedom do we have in choosing q?

Suppose NL on A satisfies 1 and 2, and define an equality relation on A thus: xEy iff $xNLy$ and $yNLx$. Then E is an equivalence relation, that is, it is reflexive,

3. $\qquad\qquad\qquad xEx,$

symmetric,

4. $\qquad\qquad\qquad xEy \rightarrow yEx,$

and transitive,

5. $\qquad\qquad\qquad (xEy \ \& \ yEz) \rightarrow xEz.$

Thus, E partitions A into equivalence classes. Let $(x) = \{y \mid xEy\}$ be x's equivalence class under E, and let D be the set of all equivalence classes of members of A. Define a greaterness relation on A thus: xGy iff $xNLy$ but not $xNLx$. G is irreflexive,

6. $\qquad\qquad\qquad -(xGx),$

and transitive,

7. $\qquad\qquad\qquad (xGy \ \& \ yGz) \rightarrow xGz.$

G and E are mutually exclusive,

8. $\qquad\qquad\qquad -(xGy \ \& \ xEy),$

but connect A,

9. $\qquad\qquad\qquad xGy \lor xEy \lor yGx.$

Conversely, given E and G on A satisfying 3–9, we may define $xNLy$ by $xGy \lor xEy$ and prove 1 and 2. It is more elegant to begin with NL, but E and G make more structure explicit.

However we start, E is a congruence relation with respect to G, that is,

10. $\qquad\qquad\qquad (xEy \ \& \ yGz) \rightarrow xGz,$
11. $\qquad\qquad\qquad (xEy \ \& \ zGy) \rightarrow zGx.$

70

To prove 11, suppose xEy and zGy. If zEx, then by 5, zEy, which violates 8, since zGy; if xGz, then by 7, xGy, which violates 8, since xEy. Hence, by 9, xGz. The proof of 10 is similar. G induces a relation $\mathcal{G}$ on D thus: $(x)\mathcal{G}(y)$ iff xGy. By 10 and 11, $\mathcal{G}$ is well defined, that is, independent of the choice of a representative from an equivalence class. $\mathcal{G}$ totally orders D. If $(x)\mathcal{G}(y)$ and $(x) = (y)$, xGy and xEy, which violates 8; thus, $\mathcal{G}$ is irreflexive. If neither $(x)\mathcal{G}(y)$ nor $(y)\mathcal{G}(x)$, then neither xGy nor yGx, so xEy by 9; thus, $(x) = (y)$, so D is strictly connected. It follows from these three facts that $\mathcal{G}$ totally orders D. Intuitively, this means that $\mathcal{G}$ arranges D in a straight line.

Sometimes we can prove the existence of a function $q: A \to R$ such that $q(x) = q(y)$ iff xEy, and xGy iff $q(x) > q(y)$. Then, given NL, there is a quantity q representing NL, or E and G, in the indicated sense. The uniqueness of q is a more delicate matter than its existence. The intuition is that the more information about members of A that has been captured by structure on A to which q must conform, the fewer ways there will be for a function q to represent this structure in R; so although q cannot be unique, we want to minimize the number of functions q by maximizing informative structure on A. NL alone leaves q badly underdetermined. Call a (partial) function g from reals to reals increasing iff for all reals a and b in its domain, $a < b$ iff $g(a) < g(b)$. Then if f represents E and G and g is an increasing function whose domain is the range of f, then $h(x) = g(f(x))$ also represents E and G; for since g is one to one, xEy iff $f(x) = f(y)$ iff $g(f(x)) = g(f(y))$ iff $h(x) = h(y)$; and since g is increasing with the range of f as its domain, xGy iff $f(x) > f(y)$ iff $g(f(x)) > g(f(y))$ iff $h(x) > h(y))$; thus, h represents G and E. As a tiny consolation, we show conversely that if f represents E and G, then $f(x) = g(q(x))$ for some increasing g whose domain is the range of q. To define g, pick a in the range of q; then $q(x) = a$ for some x in A; let $g(a) = f(x)$. If $a = g(y)$ for some other y, $q(x) = q(y)$, so since q represents E, xEy, and then since f represents E, $f(x) = f(y)$;

71

thus, g is well defined, and its domain is clearly the range of q. For x in A, $q(x) = a$ for some a; then $f(x) = g(a) = g(q(x))$, so f is the composition of g upon q. Next, pick a and b in g's domain; there are x and y such that $g(x) = a$ and $g(y) = b$. Thus, if $a < b$, $q(x) < q(y)$, so yGx, and then $g(b) = f(y) > f(x) = g(a)$, since f represents G. Conversely, if $g(b) > g(a)$, $f(y) = g(b) > g(a) = f(x)$, so yGx, and then $b = q(y) > q(x) = a$. Hence, g is increasing. It follows that a function f represents E and G iff there is an increasing g with domain the range of q and such that $f(x) = g(q(x))$. Thus, there are as many ways to represent E and G in R as there are increasing sequences of reals with as many terms as D has members. Since there are in general an enormous number of such sequences, q fails very badly to be unique.

We could shrink the class of representations if we could discern in A enough structure to leave arbitrary only the choice of q's zero and unit, that is, x and y in A such that $q(x) = 0$ and $q(y) = 1$. The Fahrenheit and centigrade temperature scales differ only in their zero and unit; all the rest is somehow fixed by the thermal facts. Algebraically, this translates into requiring that for any f that represents the structure of A, there is a positive real α and a real β such that $f(x) = \alpha q(x) + \beta$ for each x in A. Then if $q(x) = -\beta$, $f(x) = 0$, so β shifts the zero point; and if $q(x) = 1 - \beta/\alpha$, $f(x) = 1$, so α stretches or shrinks the unit. We say that f is a positive linear transformation of q iff $f(x) = \alpha q(x) + \beta$ for some positive α. If every function representing the structure on A is a positive linear transformation of q, we say that q is unique up to a positive linear transformation; in that case, the structure fixes q except for its zero and unit.

NL does force linear transformations of q to be positive; for in any nontrivial case, there are x and y in A such that xGy. If $\alpha = 0$, then $f(x) = \beta = f(y)$, so f does not represent G; and if α is negative, then since $q(x) > q(y)$, $f(x) < f(y)$, so f does not represent G. But most increasing functions of a quantity are not positive linear transformations of it. [Pick $a > 1$ and let

72

$f(x) = a^{q(x)}$; f is an increasing function of q but not linear, so we have as many examples as reals.] Hence, we have to discern more structure in A.

It will suffice to detect an operation on members of A whereby we can mix them to make a member of A that we can compare with members of A under G and E. The idea is that we choose a real number a such that $0 \le a \le 1$. We think of a as a proportion; it might be $\frac{1}{3}$ (but it need not be rational). Then for any x and y in A, we take $a = \frac{1}{3}$ of x (or something E to x) and $1 - a = \frac{2}{3}$ of y (or something E to y), and we mix them thoroughly to get a member, call it $m(a, x, y)$, of A. By 9, the mixture $m(a, x, y)$ bears a definite relation to each member of A. Consider, for example, temperature. Let A be an expandable class of equal volumes of water (say, glasses). Suppose each volume is in thermal equilibrium; that is, no part is hotter than any other. G is the relation of being hotter than, and E is the relation of being as hot as. Suppose x is hotter than y and y is hotter than z; xGy and yGz. Assume, and this is the crux, that there is a unique proportion a such that if we mix any a part of x (or anything E to x) with any $1 - a$ part of z (or anything E to z), then the mixture $m(a, x, z)$ will come to thermal equilibrium (with no heat gain by stirring in mixing and no heat loss to the mixing glass; both are idealizations) so that y is as hot as the mixture; assume, that is, that whenever xGy and yGz, there is a unique a such that $yEm(a, x, z)$. Then the proportion a tells us *where* to put y between x and z. G alone only tells us *that* y goes between x and z. But if a is close to 1, so we need a lot of x but only a little of z, y should be close below x and far above z. Mixtures tell us the "ratio" a that the distance from z to y should bear to the distance from z to x, and this information will constrain q up to the choice of its zero and unit. The idea of this use of mixtures is due to John von Neumann and Oskar Morgenstern.[1]

We next axiomatize mixtures. The function m is a three-place function whose first argument is a proportion, whose other two arguments are members of A, and whose value is a member of A. In the standard notation, $[0, 1] = \{a \in R \mid 0 \leq a \leq 1\}$ and $m: [0, 1] \times A \times A \to A$. Our axioms are as follows:

12. $\qquad\qquad\qquad m(1, x, y)Ex.$

If you mix all of x with none of y, you get x, which is equal to x.

13. $\qquad\qquad\qquad m(a, x, y)Em(1 - a, y, x).$

The mixture of a of x with $1 - a$ of y is equal to the mixture of $1 - a$ of y with $1 - (1 - a) = a$ of x. One might think these two axioms are known *a priori*, but the next is not, and that is important, because it is the *a posteriori* axioms that describe genuine structure in A.

14. $\qquad\qquad\qquad m(a, m(b, x, y), y)Em(ab, x, y).$

This axiom predicts the result of a *sequence* of two mixing operations from the original ingredients and proportions. To see what it predicts, consider mass. Let A be a class of objects any two of which have the same volume and any one of which has uniform density throughout (though different members of A may have different densities). xEy iff you have to push them equally hard to accelerate them equally; xGy iff you have to push x harder than y to accelerate them equally. A mixture $m(a, x, y)$ is made thus: take any a part of x (or something E to x) and any $1 - a$ part of y (or something E to y); this is done by volume; pulverize the parts, and blend until the mixture has uniform density; do this by comparing parts of it of equal volume by E and G. We are assuming that the mixture's volume is that of all members of A. To see what 14 says in this example, pretend that you can already measure mass in, say, grams. Suppose x has a mass of 24 g and y has a mass of 72 g. Mixing $\frac{1}{3}$ of x with $\frac{2}{3}$ of y, one would expect $m(\frac{1}{3}, x, y)$ to have mass $\frac{1}{3}(24) + \frac{2}{3}(72) = 56$. Now mixing $\frac{3}{4}$ of this mixture with $\frac{1}{4}$ of y (not what is left of y, but the original y or something E to that y), one would expect $m(\frac{3}{4}, m(\frac{1}{3}, x, y), y)$

74

to have mass $\frac{3}{4}(56) + \frac{1}{4}(72) = 60$. But suppose we had just mixed $\frac{1}{3} \times \frac{3}{4} = \frac{1}{4}$ of x with $1 - \frac{1}{4} = \frac{3}{4}$ of y; one would expect $m(\frac{1}{4}, x, y)$ to have mass $\frac{1}{4}(24) + \frac{3}{4}(72) = 60$. So one expects $m(\frac{3}{4}, m(\frac{1}{3}, x, y), y)$ to be E to $m(\frac{1}{4}, x, y)$; that is what 14 predicts. Our calculations of expected masses depend on the principle that the mass of $m(a, x, y)$ should be a times the mass of x plus 1 $- a$ times the mass of y, that is, that $q(m(a, x, y)) = aq(x) + (1 - a)q(y)$. This principle, called linearity, will follow from our axioms (though it is important that we not mention q in the axioms since they specify q-free structure in A for q to represent in R). Linearity, as its name hints, is important in making q unique up to a positive linear transformation. In the mass example, 14 requires that no mass change distinguish between whether two mixing actions are done in sequence or combined by linearity into a single action. In that limited sense, 14 says that A exhibits no "chemistry" of mass.[2] That is how 14 is *a posteriori*; that is one way q will represent *facts* about A.

We next assume a form of continuity:

15.   Suppose that $\lim a_i = a$. If $m(a_i, x, y)NLz$ for all i, then
$m(a, x, y)NLz$; and if $zNLm(a_i, x, y)$ for all i, then
$$zNLm(a, x, y).$$

To see what 15 says, suppose, for example, that no matter how small a positive part a_i of x we mix with $1 - a_i$ of y, z is heavier than the mixture $m(a_i, x, y)$. Then 15 says that though z might be as heavy as the mixture $m(0, x, y)$, this limit mixture cannot jump discontinuously to being heavier than z. Continuity principles have a seductive way with credulity; but if there can be jumps in nature, one should be wary of thinking them *a priori* or necessary. So 15 says that as a matter of fact, there are no jumps in the structure of A. The continuity principle, 15, is I. N. Herstein and John Milnor's route[3] to von Neumann and Morgenstern's intermediate proportion described earlier.

We finally make explicit the extensionality principle we have been assuming parenthetically:

16. $xEy \rightarrow m(a,x,z) \; Em(a,y,z)$.

This means that if we mix a of x with z, then the mass (say) of the mixture depends only on the *mass* of x, not on other quantities had by x independent of its mass; so had we mixed z with anything as massive as x, this second mixture should be as massive as the one we actually made. Since it is not clear that it can be known *a priori* that there are such quantities, or that any proper quantity is such, it is not clear that 16 is known *a priori*.

Axioms 12–16 with 1–2 or 3–9 suffice. That is, if A with G, E, m, and the definition of NL satisfies 3–9 and 12–16, or with NL, m, and the definitions of G and E satisfies 1–2 and 12–16, then there exists a $q: A \rightarrow R$, which represents G and E, or NL, and which satisfies linearity; and this q is unique up to a linear transformation. A proof of this fact is given in Appendix A of this chapter; it is due to von Neumann and Morgenstern, though our exposition often follows a version due to Herstein and Milnor.

How unusual is it that a quantitative structure should possess a mixture operation? That is, suppose that A is a structure with relations NL, G, and E, which satisfy 1–9 and the definitions of NL, G, and E in terms of each other; and suppose that q is a function from A to R that represents NL, E, and G. What conditions on q, NL, G, and E are necessary and sufficient for there to exist a mixture function m: $[0, 1] \times A \times A \rightarrow R$ such that 12–16 are also satisfied? Lemma 3 of Appendix A says that A must be dense under G, that is, that if xGy, then for some z in A, xGz and zGy. Combined with linearity, density suggests the following concept; let us say that intermediate q positions are occupied in A iff for every x and y in A and every a in $[0, 1]$, there is a z in A such that $q(z) = aq(x) + (1 - a) \cdot q(y)$. We can show that A possesses a mixture operation if and only if intermediate q positions are occupied; a proof of this is presented in Appendix B. It fol-

76

lows that mixture operations are exactly as common as quantities whose intermediate positions are occupied. The notion of a mixture might seem less familiar or less accessible via easy descriptive steps than the notion of a quantity whose intermediate positions are occupied. But axioms 1–12 describe a structure on A without mentioning the quantity q but in such a way that there exists a q unique up to a linear transformation that represents this structure. So it might be claimed that the axiomatization 1–12 is a noncircular analysis of quantity that exhibits (a species of) the structures of facts that quantities represent. Moreover, in some cases, it is *more* natural *first* to devise a mixture operation, and *then* to let mixtures fix a quantity up to the choice of its zero and unit, than it is to generate mixtures from the occupants of the intermediate positions of a prior quantity; this is the case, it seems, when we set out to detect a quantity in desire.

How often are a quantity's intermediate positions occupied? Consider the masses of a star and an electron in it. It is tempting to suppose that each intermediate mass is the mass of some *part* of the star more massive than the electron. But are there always such parts if, as has been suggested, fundamental particles like electrons are points, that is, lack volume? Moreover, it is not always true that if x is a proper part of y, $q(x) < q(y)$; parts of the sun may be as hot as is the sun (on average). In the case of the drop in temperature from the sun to the earth, it is tempting to suppose that heat drops off smoothly with distance, so each intermediate temperature is manifestable at some intermediate place. But we should not claim to know this *a priori*, for whether it is so depends on how heat radiates, and that we do not know *a priori*. At this point one might give up and claim that it suffices for quantity that its intermediate positions *could* be occupied, even if, in fact, they are not; if that were so, it might be one way in which unactualized possibilities sneak into natural science.

APPENDIX A: THE EXISTENCE AND UNIQUENESS, UP TO A POSITIVE LINEAR TRANSFORMATION, OF QUANTITY

Lemma 1. If $\lim a_i = a$ and $m(a_i, x, y)Ez$, then $m(a, x, y)Ez$.

Proof. By 15, $m(a, x, y)$ NLz and $zNLm(a, x, y)$, so $m(a, x, y)Ez$. ∎

Lemma 2. If $xNLy$ and $yNLz$, then there is an $a \in [0, 1]$ such that $m(a, x, z)Ey$.

Proof. Let $T = \{a | m(a, x, z)NLy\}$. By 15, T is a closed subset of $[0,1]$. $m(1, x, z)ExNLy$, so $1 \in T$, so T is not empty. Similarly, $W = \{a | yNLm(a, x, z)\}$ is a closed subset of $[0, 1]$ and $0 \in W$. By 2, $[0,1] = T \cup W$. But $[0,1]$ is connected; it cannot be the union of closed, disjoint, nonempty sets. Hence, some number c is a member of both T and W. Then $m(c, x, z)NLy$ and $yNLm(c, x, z)$, so $m(c, x, z)Ey$. ∎

Scholium. This is Herstein and Milnor's proof. If xEy and yEz, any $a \in [0,1]$ will do.

Lemma 3. If xGy and $0 < a < 1$, then $xGm(a, x, y)$ and $m(a, x, y)Gy$.

Proof. Suppose $m(a, x, y)NLx$. Then by lemma 2, $xEm(b, m(a, x, y), y)$ for some b. By axiom 14, $m(b, m(a, x, y), y)Em(ba, x, y)$, so $xEm(ba, x, y)$. Let $T = \{b | xEm(ba, x, y)\}$; we have shown T nonempty. By lemma 1, T is closed. If $0 \in T$, $xEm(0, x, y)Em(1, y, x)Ey$, so xEy, which is impossible, since xGy. Hence, $0 \notin T$, so since T is closed, 0 is not a limit point of T. But 0 is a lower bound for T and T is not empty, so it has a greatest lower bound b_0. Since 0 is not a limit point of T, $b_0 > 0$. Since T is closed, $b_0 \in T$, so $xEm(b_0a, x, y)$. Then by axiom 16, $m(a, x, y)$ is E to $m(a, m(b_0a, x, y), y)$; but $m(a, m(b_0a, x, y), y)Em(a^2b_0x, y)$; so $m(a^2b_0, x, y)Em(a, x, y)$. Since $m(a, x, y)NLx$, $m(a^2b_0, x, y)NLx$ and $xNLy$ (since xGy), so by

78

lemma 2, for some $c, xEm(c, m(a^2b_0, x, y), y)Em(a^2b_0c, x, y)$. If $c = 0, xEm(0, x, y)E(1, y, x)Ey$, so since xGy, $c > 0$. But since $0 < a < 1$ and $b_0 > 0$, $ab_0c < b_0$. Thus, ab_0c is a member of T less than b_0, which is impossible. Hence, $xGm(a, x, y)$; and similarly, $m(a, x, y)Gy$. ∎

Scholium. Thus, A is dense with respect to G.

Lemma 4. If xGy, then $m(a, x, y)Gm(b, x, y)$ iff $a > b$.

Proof. Suppose $1 > a > b > 0$. Since $1 > a > 0$ and xGy, $m(a, x, y)Gy$. Since $a > b > 0$, $1 > b/a > 0$, so $m(a, x, y)Gm(b/a, m(a, x, y), y)Em(b, x, y)$, so $m(a, x, y)Gm(b, x, y)$. If $a = 1$ and $b = 0$, $m(a, x, y)Ex$ and $m(b, x, y)Em(1, y, x)Ey$, so since xGy, $m(a, x, y)Gm(b, x, y)$. If $a = 1$ and $b > 0$, $m(a, x, y)ExGm(0, x, y)$. If $a < 1$ and $b = 0$, $m(a, x, y)GyEm(1, y, x)Em(b, x, y)$.

Suppose conversely that $b \geq a$. If $b = a$, then $m(a, x, y) = m(b, x, y)$, so $m(a, x, y)Em(b, x, y)$, so it is not true that $m(a, x, y)Gm(b, x, y)$. If $b > a$, then by the first paragraph of this proof, $m(b, x, y)Gm(a, x, y)$, so not-$(m(a, x, y)Gm(b, x, y))$ again. ∎

Lemma 5. If xGy and yGz, then there is a unique a such that $yEm(a, x, z)$.

Proof. By lemma 2, there is at least one. Suppose there were two, say $a > b$. By lemma 4, $m(a, x, z)Gm(b, x, z)$. But y must be E to both mixtures, so they must be E to each other, which is impossible. ∎

Scholium. This is the intermediate value property of mixtures.

Definition. If xGy, let $S_{xy} = \{z \in A | xNLz \& zNLy\}$. For each $z \in S_{xy}$, let $f_{xy}(z)$ be the unique $a \in [0,1]$ such that $zEm(a, x, y)$.

Lemma 6. For all $z, w \in S_{xy}$, $f_{xy}(z) > f_{xy}(w)$ iff zGw, and $f_{xy}(z) = f_{xy}(w)$ iff zEw.

Proof. The first part is lemma 4. For the second, if $f_{xy}(z) = f_{xy}(w)$, $zEm(f_{xy}(z), x, y)Em(f_{xy}(w), x, y)Ew$; and if zEw, then $m(f_{xy}(w), x, y)EwEz$, so $f_{xy}(z) = f_{xy}(w)$. ∎

Scholium. Thus, f_{xy} represents G and E restricted to S_{xy}.

If there are not $x, y \in A$ such that xGy, then xEy always. Then let $f(x) = 0$ for all x in A; f represents G and E. Since all and only the constant functions represent G and E, and they are linear transformations of f, f is unique up to a linear transformation. To avoid this trivial case, we shall assume from now on that for some x and y, xGy.

Suppose A were S_{xy} for some $x, y \in A$, that is, that A had a top and a bottom. (That would happen if A were the closure of a finite set under mixing.) Then f_{xy} would suffice as the quantity we require. But we have no right to assume in general that A has a top or a bottom. We shall instead fix $r_0, r_1 \in A$ such that $r_1 G r_0$. We will arbitrarily let r_0 be the zero point; and $S_{r_1 r_0}$ will be the "interval" in A whose "length" we will take as the unit for each S_{xy}. We must then show that such normalizations of the f_{xy}'s, one for each S_{xy} (the "finite" intervals of A), can be fitted together into a single quantity defined for all of A.

But before beginning this project, we must first prove a lemma that might seem obviously true but that seems surprisingly complex to prove.

Lemma 7. $xEm(a, x, x)$.

Proof. Let $T = \{a | m(a, x, x)Gx\}$ and suppose $a \in T$. Then $0 < a < 1$. Pick any c such that $0 < c < a$. Then $0 < c/a < 1$; write $b = c/a$. Since $a \in T$, $m(a, x, x)Gx$, so by lemma 3, $m(ba, x, x)$ $Em(b, m(a, x, x), x)Gx$, and $m(a, x, x)Gm(b, m(a, x, x), x)Em(ba,$

$x, x)$, so $c = ba \in T$ and $m(a, x, x)Gm(c, x, x)$. Now pick any c such that $a < c < 1$. $m(a, x, x)E(1 - a, x, x)$, so $1 - a \in T$. $0 < 1 - c < 1 - a$, so as before, $1 - c \in T$ and $m(1 - a, x, x)Gm(1 - c, x, x)$. Then since $m(1 - c, x, x)Em(c, x, x)$, $c \in T$ and $m(a, x, x)Gm(c, x, x)$.

So if T is not empty, we may pick $a \in T$, and then for any $b \neq a$ such that $0 < b < 1$, $m(a, x, x)Gm(b, x, x)$. But $b \in T$, $a \neq b$, and $0 < a < 1$, so symmetrically, $m(b, x, x)Gm(a, x, x)$ also, which is impossible. Thus, T is empty, and similarly, so is $\{a | xGm(a, x, x)\}$. ∎

Lemma 8. If xGy, then (a) $f_{xy}(y) = 0$; (b) $f_{xy}(x) = 1$; (c) if $0 < b < 1$ and $xNLzGy$, then $f_{xy}(m(b, z, y)) = bf_{xy}(z)$; (d) if $0 < b < 1$ and $xGzNLy$, then $f_{xy}(m(b, z, x)) = 1 - b + bf_{xy}(z)$; and (e) if f is a real-valued function whose domain includes S_{xy} and that satisfies (a), (b), and (c) or (d), then f restricted to S_{xy} is f_{xy}.

Proof. Parts (a) and (b) are obvious. If zEx, $f_{xy}(z) = f_{xy}(x) = 1$ and $m(b, z, y)Em(b, x, y)$, so $f_{xy}(m(b, z, y)) = f_{xy}(m(b, x, y)) = b = bf_{xy}(z)$. If xGz, let $a = f_{xy}(z)$; $zEm(a, x, y)$, so $m(b, z, y)$ $Em(b, m(a, x, y), y)Em(ba, x, y)$, so $f_{xy}(m(b, z, y)) = ba = bf_{xy}(z)$, which proves (c). If zEy, $f_{xy}(z) = f_{xy}(y) = 0$ and $m(b, z, x)Em(b, y, x)Em(1 - b, x, y)$, so $f_{xy}(m(b, z, x)) = 1 - b = 1 - b + bf_{xy}(z)$. If zGy, let $a = f_{xy}(z)$; $zEm(a, x, y)E(1 - a, y, x)$, so $m(b, z, x)Em(b, m(1 - a, y, x), x)$ $Em(b(1 - a), y, x)Em(1 - b(1 - a), x, y)$, so $f_{xy}(m(b, z, x)) = 1 - b + ba = 1 - b + bf_{xy}(z)$, which proves (d).

Let $\mathcal{S}_{xy} = \{(z) | z \in S_{xy}\} \subseteq D$ and define $F_{xy} : \mathcal{S}_{xy} \to R$ by $F_{xy}((z)) = f_{xy}(z)$. By lemma 4, F_{xy} is one-one. For $b \in [0, 1]$, $f_{xy}(m(b, x, y)) = b$. Hence, F_{xy} maps $\mathcal{S}_{xy}$ one-one onto $[0, 1]$. Thus, F_{xy} has an inverse $\psi : [0, 1] \to \mathcal{S}_{xy}$. Define $F : \mathcal{S}_{xy} \to R$ by $F((z)) = f(z)$ and $\phi : [0, 1] \to R$ by $\phi(a) = F(\psi(a))$. $F_{xy}((x)) = f_{xy}(x) = 1$ and $F_{xy}((y)) = f_{xy}(y) = 0$, so $\psi(1) = (x)$ and $\psi(0) = (y)$, so since f satisfies (a) and (b), $\phi(0) = F(\psi(0)) = F((y)) = f(y) = 0$, and $\phi(1) = F(\psi(1)) = F((x)) = f(x) = 1$.

Suppose f satisfies (c). $\phi(ba) = F(\psi(ba)) = F((m(ba, x, y))) =$

81

$F((m(b, m(a, x, y), y)))$. If $0 < a, b < 1$, $m(a, x, y)Gy$, so by (c), $F((m(b, m(a, x, y), y))) = bF((m(a, x, y))) = bF(\psi(a)) = b\phi(a)$, so $\phi(ba) = b\phi(a)$. If $a = 0$, $\phi(ab) = \phi(0) = 0 = b \cdot 0 = b\phi(a)$. If $a = 1$, $m(a, x, y)Ex$, so $m(b, m(a, x, y), y)Em(b, x, y)$; then by (c) since xGy, $F((m(b, x, y))) = bF((x)) = b \cdot 1 = b\phi(a)$. Hence, if $a \in [0, 1]$ and $0 < b < 1$, $\phi(ab) = b\phi(a)$.

Suppose f satisfies (d). $\phi(1 - b + ba) = F(\psi(1 - b + ba)) = F((m(1 - b + ba, x, y))) = F((m(b, m(a, x, y), x)))$. If $0 < a, b < 1$, then since xGy, $xGm(a, x, y)$, so by (d), $F((m, (b, m(a, x, y), x))) = 1 - b + bF((m(a, x, y)) = 1 - b + bF(\psi(a)) = 1 - b + b\phi(a)$, so $\phi(1 - b + ba) = 1 - b + b\phi(a)$. If $a = 0$, $\phi(1 - b + ba) = \phi(1 - b) = F(\psi(1 - b)) = F((m(1 - b, x, y))) = F((m(b, y, x)))$; but xGy, so by (d) $F((m(b, y, x))) = 1 - b + bF((y)) = 1 - b = 1 - b + b \cdot 0 = 1 - b + b\phi(a)$. If $a = 1$, $\phi(1 - b + ba) = \phi(1) = 1 = 1 - b + b \cdot 1 = 1 - b + b\phi(a)$. Hence, if $a \in [0, 1]$ and $0 < b < 1$, $\phi(1 - b + ba) = 1 - b + b\phi(a)$.

Hence, since f satisfies (c) or (d), if $a \in [0, 1]$ and $0 < b < 1$, $\phi(ab) = b\phi(a)$ or $\phi(1 - b + ba) = 1 - b + b\phi(a)$. In the first case, taking $a = 1$, $\phi(b) = b\phi(1) = b$. In the second case, if $0 < b < 1$, $0 < 1 - b < 1$, and taking $a = 0$, $\phi(b) = \phi(1 - (1 - b) + (1 - b)a) = 1 - (1 - b) + (1 - b)\phi(0) = b$. Hence, if $0 < b < 1$, $\phi(b) = b$. But $\phi(0) = 0$ and $\phi(1) = 1$. So $\phi(b) = b$ for all $b \in [0, 1]$. Hence, ψ, the inverse of F_{xy}, is also an inverse of F. Thus, since inverses are unique, F is F_{xy}, so the restriction of f to S_{xy} is f_{xy}. ∎

Definition. For any reals α, β such that $\alpha > \beta$, define $g_{xy}^{\alpha\beta}$: $S_{xy} \to R$ by $g_{xy}^{\alpha\beta}(z) = (\alpha - \beta)f_{xy}(z) + \beta$.

Scholium. $g_{xy}^{\alpha\beta}$ changes the scale of f_{xy} by shifting its zero and unit.

Lemma 9. If xGy, then (a) $g_{xy}^{\alpha\beta}(y) = \beta$; (b) $g_{xy}^{\alpha\beta}(x) = \alpha$; (c) $g_{xy}^{\alpha\beta}$ represents G and E restricted to S_{xy}; (d) if $0 < b < 1$ and $xNLzGy$, $g_{xy}^{\alpha\beta}(m(b, z, y)) = bg_{xy}^{\alpha\beta}(z) + (1 - b)\beta$; (e) if $0 < b < 1$

82

and $xGzNLy$, $g_{xy}^{\alpha\beta}(m(b,z,x)) = bg_{xy}^{\alpha\beta}(z) + (1 - b)\alpha$; and (f) if g is a real-valued function whose domain includes S_{xy} and that satisfies (a), (b), and (d) or (e), then g restricted to S_{xy} is $g_{xy}^{\alpha\beta}$.

Proof. Parts (a) and (b) are immediate from lemma 8(a) and (b). Since $\alpha > \beta$, $g_{xy}^{\alpha\beta}$ is an increasing function of f_{xy}, so (c) follows from lemma 6. Parts (d) and (e) come from lemma 8(c) and (d) by simple algebra. If g satisfies (a), (b), and (d) or (e), then $f(z) = (g(z) - \beta)/(\alpha - \beta)$ satisfies the hypotheses of lemma 8(e), so f restricted to S_{xy} is f_{xy}, so g restricted to s_{xy} is $g_{xy}^{\alpha\beta}$. ∎

Lemma 10. Pick $z \in S_{xy}$ and let $g_{xy}^{\alpha\beta}(z) = \gamma$. If zGy, then if $w \in S_{zy} \subseteq S_{xy}$, $g_{xy}^{\alpha\beta}(w) = g_{zy}^{\gamma\beta}(w)$; if xGy, then if $w \in S_{xz} \subseteq S_{xy}$, $g_{xy}^{\alpha\beta}(w) = g_{xz}^{\alpha\gamma}(w)$.

Proof. If zGy, $\gamma > \beta$ by 9(c). $g_{xy}^{\alpha\beta}(\gamma) = \beta$ by 9(a) and $g_{xy}^{\alpha\beta}(z) = \gamma$, so $g_{xy}^{\alpha\beta}$ satisfies 9(a) and (b), since $g_{zy}^{\gamma\beta}(z) = \gamma$. If $zNLwGy$ and $0 < b < 1$, then $g_{xy}^{\alpha\beta}(m(b,w,\gamma)) = bg_{xy}^{\alpha\beta}(w) + (1 - b)\beta$ by 9(d), so $g_{xy}^{\alpha\beta}$ satisfies 9(d). So by 9(f), $g_{xy}^{\alpha\beta}$ restricted to S_{xy} is $g_{zy}^{\gamma\beta}$, as required. The other claim is symmetric using 9(e) in place of 9(d). ∎

Lemma 11. If $xNLzGwNLy$, $\alpha_i = g_{xy}^{\alpha\beta}(z)$ and $\beta_i = g_{xy}^{\alpha\beta}(w)$, then $g_{xy}^{\alpha\beta}$ restricted to S_{zw} is $g_{zw}^{\alpha_i\beta_i}$.

Proof. $g_{xy}^{\alpha\beta}$ restricted to S_{zy} is $g_{zy}^{\alpha_i\beta}$ by lemma 10. Thus, $\beta_i = g_{xy}^{\alpha\beta}(w) = g_{zy}^{\alpha_i\beta}(w)$, so by 10 again, $g_{zy}^{\alpha_i\beta}$ restricted to S_{zw} is $g_{zw}^{\alpha_i\beta_i}$. Hence, $g_{xy}^{\alpha\beta}$ restricted to S_{zw} is $g_{zw}^{\alpha_i\beta_i}$. ∎

Definition. Fix $r_0, r_1 \in A$ such that r_1Gr_0.

Lemma 12. If $r_0, r_1 \in S_{xy}$, there is a unique $g_{xy}^{\alpha_0\beta_0}$ such that $g_{xy}^{\alpha_0\beta_0}(r_0) = 0$ and $g_{xy}^{\alpha_0\beta_0}(r_1) = 1$.

Proof. $g_{xy}^{\alpha\beta}(r_0) = 0$ and $g_{xy}^{\alpha\beta}(r_1) = 1$ iff both

$$(\beta - \alpha)f_{xy}(r_0) + \beta = 0,$$

$$(\beta - \alpha)f_{xy}(r_1) + \beta = 1.$$

These two simultaneous equations have a unique solution α_0, β_0 (one such solution for each x,y). By lemma 6, $f_{xy}(r_1) > f_{xy}(r_0)$, so $\alpha_0 > \beta_0$. Hence, by lemma 9, $g_{xy}^{\alpha_0\beta_0}$ exists and is unique. ∎

Definition. If $r_0, r_1 \in S_{xy}$, let h_{xy} be the unique $g_{xy}^{\alpha_0\beta_0}$ guaranteed by lemma 12.

Lemma 13. If $r_0, r_1 \in S_{zw} \subseteq S_{xy}$, then h_{xy} restricted to S_{zw} is h_{zw}.

Proof. Let $\alpha_i = h_{xy}(z)$ and $\beta_i = h_{xy}(w)$. By lemma 11, h_{xy} restricted to S_{zw} is $g_{zw}^{\alpha_i\beta_i}$. Hence, $g_{zw}^{\alpha_i\beta_i}(r_0) = h_{xy}(r_0) = 0$ and $g_{zw}^{\alpha_i\beta_i}(r_1) = h_{xy}(r_1) = 1$, so by lemma 12, $g_{zw}^{\alpha_i\beta_i}$ is h_{zw}. Thus, h_{xy} restricted to S_{zw} is h_{zw}. ∎

Lemma 14. For every z there are x,y such that $z, r_0, r_1 \in S_{xy}$ and for any x', y', if $z, r_0, r_1 \in S_{x'y'}$, $h_{xy}(z) = h_{x'y'}(z)$.

Proof. Let y be r_0 if $zNLr_0$ and z otherwise; let x be z if $zNLr_1$ and r_1 otherwise. Then $z, r_0, r_1 \in S_{xy}$. Suppose $z, r_0, r_1 \in S_{x'y'}$. Let u be the greater of x, x', and v, the lesser of y, y'. Then $z, r_0, r_1 \in S_{xy} \subseteq S_{uv}$ and $z, r_0, r_1 \in S_{x'y'} \subseteq S_{uv}$, so by lemma 13, $h_{xy}(z) = h_{uv}(z) = h_{x'y'}(z)$. ∎

Definition. Let q be the union of the h_{xy} for all x,y such that $r_0, r_1 \in S_{xy}$.

Lemma 15. If zGw, $\alpha = q(z)$ and $\beta = q(w)$, then $\alpha > \beta$ and q restricted to S_{zw} is $g_{zw}^{\alpha\beta}$.

Proof. Let x be the greater of r_1, z, and y, the lesser of r_0, w; then $z, w, r_0, r_1 \in S_{xy}$. h_{xy} is $g_{xy}^{\alpha_0\beta_0}$ for some unique α_0, β_0; by lemma 14, q restricted to S_{xy} is h_{xy} and thus $g_{xy}^{\alpha_0\beta_0}$. Hence, $g_{xy}^{\alpha_0\beta_0}(z) = h_{xy}(z) = q(z) = \alpha$ and $g_{xy}^{\alpha_0\beta_0}(w) = h_{xy}(w) = q(w) = \beta$. Since $g_{xy}^{\alpha_0\beta_0}$ represents G and E restricted to S_{xy}, $\alpha > \beta$. By lemma 11, $g_{xy}^{\alpha_0\beta_0}$ restricted to S_{zw} is $g_{zw}^{\alpha\beta}$, so q restricted to S_{zw} is $g_{zw}^{\alpha\beta}$.

Lemma 16. q represents G and E.

Proof. If xGy, $q(x) > q(y)$ by lemma 15. If $q(x) > q(y)$, then $g_{xy}^{q(x)q(y)}$ $(x) = h_{xy}(x) > h_{xy}(y) = g_{xy}^{q(x)q(y)}$ so xGy since h_{xy} represents G restricted to S_{xy}. Thus, xGy iff $q(x) > q(y)$. Suppose xEy. Let z be the greater of x and r_1, and w, the lesser of y and r_0. Then $q(x) = h_{zw}(x) = h_{zw}(y) = q(y)$. If $q(x) = q(y)$, $h_{zw}(x) = h_{zw}(y)$, so xEy. ∎

Lemma 17. If $0 < b < 1$ and zGw, then $q(m(b,z,w)) = bq(z) + (1 - b)q(w)$.

Proof. Let $q(z) = \alpha$ and $q(w) = \beta$. By lemma 15, q restricted to S_{zw} is $g_{zw}^{\alpha\beta}$. Since zGw and $0 < b < 1$, by lemma 9(d), $g_{zw}^{\alpha\beta}(m(b,z,w)) = bg_{zw}^{\alpha\beta}(z) + (1 - b)\beta = bg_{zw}^{\alpha\beta}(z) + (1 - b)g_{zw}^{\alpha\beta}(w)$, so $q(m(b,z,w)) = bq(z) + (1 - b)q(w)$. ∎

Lemma 18. For all $a \in [0,1]$ and $x,y \in A$, $q(m(a,x,y)) = aq(x) + (1 - a)q(y)$.

Proof. If $a = 1$, $m(a,x,y)Ex$, so $q(m(a,x,y)) = q(x) = aq(x) + (1 - a)q(y)$. If $a = 0$, $m(a,x,y)Em(1 - a,y,x)Ey$, so $q(m(a,x,y)) = q(y) = aq(x) + (1 - a)q(y)$. Suppose $0 < a < 1$. If xGy, the claim is lemma 17. If yGx, $0 < 1 - a < 1$, and $q(m(a,x,y)) = q(m(1 - a,y,x)) = (1 - a)q(y) + (1 - (1 - a))q(x) = aq(x) + (1 - a)q(y)$. If xEy, then by lemma 7, $yEm(a,y,y)Em(a,x,y)$, so $q(m(a,x,y)) = q(y) = aq(x) + q(y) - aq(y)$ [for $q(x) = q(y)$ since xEy] $= aq(x) + (1 - a)q(y)$. ∎

Scholium. Thus, q is linear.

Lemma 19. For any $f: A \rightarrow R$, f is linear and represents G and E iff f is a positive linear transformation of q.

Proof. Any positive linear transformation of q is an increasing function of q and thus represents G and E. And if $f(x) = \alpha q(x) + \beta$, then

$$
\begin{aligned}
f(m(a,x,y)) &= \alpha q(m(a,x,y)) + \beta \\
&= \alpha(aq(x) + (1-a)q(y)) + \beta \\
&= a(\alpha q(x) + \beta) + (1-a)(\alpha q(y) + \beta) \\
&= af(x) + (1-a)f(y),
\end{aligned}
$$

so f is linear.

Suppose conversely that $f\colon A \to R$ is linear and represents G and E. Let

$$
\begin{aligned}
d(x,y,z) &= q(x)f(y) + q(y)f(z) + q(z)f(x) \\
&\quad - (q(x)f(z) + q(y)f(x) + q(z)f(y))
\end{aligned}
$$

(d is a determinant). We show that $d(x,y,z) = 0$ for all x,y,z. If two bear E to each other, say xEz, then $f(x) = f(z)$ and $q(x) = q(z)$, and by algebra, $d(x,y,z) = 0$. Suppose no two bear E to one another, say $xGyGz$. Then by lemma 2, there is an $a \in [0,1]$ such that $yEm(a,x,z)$, and by linearity, $f(y) = af(x) + (1-a)f(z)$ and $q(y) = aq(x) + (1-a)q(z)$; then $d(x,y,z) = 0$, again by algebra.

Pick x,y such that xGy. For all $z, d(x,y,z) = 0$, so for all z

$$
f(z) = \frac{f(x) - f(y)}{q(x) - q(y)}q(z) + \frac{f(y)q(x) - f(x)q(y)}{q(x) - q(y)},
$$

where, since xGy, $q(x) > q(y)$, so $q(x) - q(y) > 0$, so the quotients are well defined. Since xGy, $f(x) > f(y)$, so $f(x) - f(y) > 0$, so

$$
\frac{f(x) - f(y)}{q(x) - q(y)}
$$

is a positive constant. Hence, f is a positive linear transformation of q. ∎

Theorem. There exists a quantity $q\colon A \to R$, which represents E and G, which is linear on mixtures, and which is unique up to a positive linear transformation.

86

APPENDIX B: MIXTURES AND FULL MIDDLES

Let $\langle A, NL, E, G \rangle$ be a model for axioms 1–9 and the definitions of NL, E, and G in terms of one another. Say that m: $[0,1] \times A \times A \rightarrow A$ mixes A iff $\langle A, NL, E, G, m \rangle$ is a model for axioms 12–16 as well. Say that A fills the middle positions of a function $f: A \rightarrow R$ iff for each $a \in [0,1]$ and $x, y, \in A$, there is a $z \in A$ such that $f(z) = af(x) + (1 - a)f(y)$. We are to prove that A fills the middle positions of a representation of NL, E, and G iff there is a function that mixes A.

The argument of Appendix A shows that if m mixes A, there exists a linear q that represents NL, E, and G. Given $a \in [0,1]$ and $x, y \in A$, $m(a, x, y) \in A$, and by linearity, $q(m(a, x, y)) = aq(x) + (1 - a)q(y)$. Thus, A fills (with mixtures) the middle positions of the representation q of NL, E, and G.

Suppose conversely that A fills the middle positions of a representation f of NL, E and G. Define a four-place relation R such that $R(x, y, a, z)$ iff $x, y, z \in A$, $a \in [0,1]$ and $f(z) = af(x) + (1 - a)f(y)$. Since A fills f's middle positions, for any (appropriate) x, y, a, there is a z such that $R(x, y, a, z)$; and if $R(x, y, a, z)$ and $R(x, y, a, z')$, then $f(z) = af(x) + (1 - a)f(y) = f(z')$. Hence, by the axiom of choice, there is a function m: $[0,1] \times A \times A \rightarrow A$ such that for all $x, y, a, R(x, y, a, m(a, x, y))$, and thus $f(m(a, x, y)) = af(x) + (1 - a)f(y)$. We show that m mixes A. $f(m(1, x, y)) = 1f(x) + 0f(y) = f(x)$, so $xEm(1, x, y)$; thus, axiom 12 holds. $f(m(a, x, y)) = af(x) + (1 - a)f(y) = (1 - a)f(y) + (1 - (1 - a))f(x) = f(m(1 - a, y, x))$, so $m(a, x, y)Em(1 - a, y, x)$, so axiom 13 holds. $f(m(a, m(b, x, y), y)) = af(m(b, x, y)) + (1 - a)f(y) = a(bf(x) + (1 - b)f(y)) + (1 - a)f(y) = abf(x) + (1 - ab)f(y) = f(m(ab, x, y))$, so $m(a, m(b, x, y), y) Em(ab, x, y)$, so axiom 14 holds. If xEy, $f(x) = f(y)$, so $f(m(a, x, z)) = af(x) + (1 - a)f(z) = af(y) + (1 - a)f(z) = f(m(a, y, z))$, so $m(a, x, z)Em(a, y, z)$, so axiom 16 holds.

Assume that $\lim a_i = a$. Suppose that $m(a_i, x, y)NLz$ for all i. Since A fills the middle positions of f, there are $z_i \in A$ such

87

that $f(z_i) = a_i f(x) + (1 - a_i)f(y)$, and there is a $z^* \in A$ such that $f(z^*) = af(x) + (1 - a)f(y)$. But

$$
\begin{aligned}
|f(z^*) - f(z_i)| &= |(af(x) + (1 - a)f(y)) \\
&\quad - (a_i f(x) + (1 - a_i)f(y))| \\
&= |(a - a_i)f(x) + (a_i - a)f(y)|,
\end{aligned}
$$

so as $a_i \rightarrow a$, $f(z_i) \rightarrow f(z^*)$. But

$$
\begin{aligned}
f(z_i) &= a_i f(x) + (1 - a_i)f(y) \\
&= f(m(a_i, x, y)) \\
&\geq f(z),
\end{aligned}
$$

so $f(z)$ is a lower bound for the numbers $f(z_i)$. Hence, $f(z^*) \geq f(z)$. Thus, $m(a, x, y)Ez^*NLz$. Similarly, if $zNLm(a_i, x, y)$, $zNLm(a, x, y)$. Hence, axiom 15 holds, and thus m mixes A.

7

Desire

One idea of utility is that it should be the quantity of a person's desire. Can we discern in a person's appetites a class of objects on which there are binary relations and a three-place function that satisfy the axioms of the previous chapter? If so, then for each person there will exist a quantity, unique except for its zero point and its unit length, of his desire. John von Neumann and Oskar Morgenstern argued that such quantities exist.

It is easiest to begin with the greaterness and equality relations. Fix a single, hypothetical individual person in your mind, and call the members of the set we need alternatives; we shall have to be more explicit shortly about what an alternative is. The idea is that the greaterness relation should be the person's preferences among the alternatives and that the equality relation should be his indifference between them. How reasonable is it to suppose that a person's preferences and indifference satisfy axioms 3–9?

We can get some insight into the nature of alternatives if we look first at axiom 9, connectivity. Write P for the individual's preference and I for his indifference; so long as we are treating only one person, explicit mention of him is superfluous, but when people other than our individual i are at issue, we should keep him in mind by calling his preference P_i and his indifference I_i.

Connectivity then requires that

9D. $$x P_i y \lor x I_i y \lor y P_i x ,$$

that is i can, as it were, compare any two alternatives. But as the proverb has it, you cannot compare chalk with cheese; so must we conclude that preference and indifference are disconnected?

This objection assumes that chalk and cheese are alternatives. But suppose that i's choice is not between parcels of the materials (substances, stuffs) chalk and cheese, but between courses of action. He might be deciding between eating cheese and eating chalk, or between writing on a blackboard with chalk or writing on it with cheese. In either case, it is reasonable to suppose that he would have decided preferences. The upshot is that we would do well to parse both an individual's preference and his indifference as binary propositional attitudes. It is then natural to describe the alternatives as propositions. It is a good idea to say no more about propositions than the facts compel one to say; you may think of them as sentences, statements, thoughts, or possible situations, states of affairs, facts, or courses of action.

It is in i's interest that he be able to compare the various courses of action open to him. For doing so increases his chances of arranging them in a linear order, seeing what comes out on top, and thus deciding what he most wants, or is least unwilling, should be the case. Where i is unable to compare, neither can he make a rational choice and act on it. Since it is in his interest that he be able to act rationally, it is in his interest that he be able to compare alternatives. That this is in i's interest is sometimes expressed by saying that utility incorporates a normative conception of preference and indifference. But the relevant norms are not those of duty or of virtue and vice; we are not asking whether i has a duty to prefer poetry to noughts and crosses. Instead, the relevant norms are those of prudence, that is, of what is sometimes called rational self-interest. (This does not mean greed or selfishness; it is natural for rationally self-interested people to like at least a few other people and to wish them well.) Since we are thinking of prudent desires that need not be dutiful wishes, one might say that utility incorporates a conception of rational appetites.

The relevant sort of rationality has to do with the structure (as indicated by axioms 3–9) of the appetites, not with their contents, the objects of the underlying propositional attitudes; it would not be an irrationality of the relevant sort to prefer bending all straight pins above all other alternatives. One might think of the rationality of the appetites as analogous to the rigidity of those mythical bodies one studies in elementary mechanics. Both are theoretical idealizations that enable the understanding to get started. It may then be possible to grasp messy reality by comparing it with the ideal.

Even so, we do not know *a priori* that i will be able to compare some new possible course of action with all those between which in pairs he has formed decided preferences. If so, leave that proposition out of the range of alternatives on which we are specifying i's desires; i's utility for this range of alternatives will not be defined for that proposition. (If there were more than one such range, no two of them overlapping and each of them large enough, i might turn out to have more than one utility function.) The point is that where 9D fails for rational preference between propositions, we may still save 9D by shrinking the range of alternatives to one for which 9D holds; but this defense is worthwhile only if the shrunken range is large enough to be of interest. It is in i's interest that it be as large as possible; but there is no knowing *a priori* how large it will be.

Axiom 3D requires that i be indifferent between any alternative and that alternative itself; since there is nothing to choose between an alternative and itself, it is rational that i should be indifferent between "them." Axiom 4D requires that when i is indifferent between x and y, then he is indifferent between y and x; it might be thought that we have all but built a belief in the symmetry of indifference into the gram-

91

mar of "indifference between x and y" since that phrase makes it difficult to distinguish the symmetry of indifference from the symmetry of conjunction.

There are standard counterexamples to axiom 5D, the transitivity of indifference. Where i cannot tell alternatives apart, he may well be indifferent between them even though they are different. Suppose, for example, that you like beer but that (without special devices) you cannot tell the difference between a (reasonably large) glass of beer and a glass with one one-thousandth of a pint more beer. Let alternative a_0 be that you get a full pint of beer, and for each $n < 1,000$, let a_{n+1} be that you get as much beer as under a_n plus one one-thousandth more. Then since for each $n < 1,000$, you cannot tell the difference between a_n and a_{n+1}, you may well (so the story goes) be indifferent between a_n and a_{n+1}. If you were, it would follow from the transitivity of indifference that you were indifferent between a_0 and $a_{1,000}$, that is, between getting one pint of beer and two; but if you like beer, that surely need not be true.

Alfred F. MacKay[1] judges this counterexample to be superficial. Such intransitivity of indifference as it exhibits is consequent upon an intransitivity in powers of perceptual discrimination. There may well be intrinsic and serious failures of transitivity in our capacities to distinguish different things; but if so, it seems more a datum for the theory of the senses than for the theory of the appetites. There are special devices with which you could discriminate between one pint of beer and one plus one one-thousandth pints of beer, and if you really do like beer and prefer more of it to less (though not necessarily to be drunk all at once), you would prefer the second to the first rather than be indifferent between them. Hence, in order to ease understanding's grasp, the transitivity of indifference seems to be a legitimate theoretical idealization. We may conclude that we may approximate indifference as an equivalence relation.

Axiom 6D requires that i prefer no alternative to itself,

and that seems sensible enough. Axiom 7D requires that his preference be transitive and, like the transitivity of indifference, has prompted a search for counterexamples.[2] There are complex examples here that are interesting for probability theory but whose relevance to the transitivity of preference emerges, perhaps, from a simpler and more familiar case. Consider the children's game scissors–paper–stone under the rules of which the hand held flat (paper) covers, and so beats, the fist (stone), which breaks, and so beats, two extended and separated fingers (scissors), which cut, and so beat, paper. The idea of the counterexample would seem to be as follows: (a) given an opponent who presents a stone, you would rather present paper than scissors; (b) given paper, you would rather scissors than stone; but (c) given scissors, you would rather stone than paper. On first hearing, that might sound like a case in which it would be rational to prefer (a) to (b), (b) to (c), but (c) to (a), that is, a case of rational intransitive preference.

But as the shifting clauses about what is given intimate, this putative counterexample seems to trade on a confused specification of the range of alternatives. Consider these propositions:

x_1: He presents stone and you present paper.
x_2: He presents stone and you present scissors.
y_1: He presents paper and you present scissors.
y_2: He presents paper and you present stone.
z_1: He presents scissors and you present stone.
z_2: He presents scissors and you present paper.

Assuming that you want to win, it is rational that x_1Px_2, y_1Py_2, and z_1Pz_2. The grammar of (a), (b), and (c), that is, the temptation to "simplify" the given-clauses away and to treat your preferences as among three objects rather than six propositions, might seduce you into supposing obscurely something like x_2NLy_1 and y_2NLz_1, in which case there would be a genuine intransitivity. But the supposition will not survive

93

critical scrutiny; for granted that you want to win, then $x_1Py_2, x_1Pz_2, y_1Px_2, y_1Pz_2, z_1Px_2, z_1Py_2$, and probably, $x_1Iy_1Iz_1$ and $x_2Iy_2Iz_2$ (if all you care about is winning). If all the alternatives subscripted with 1 are indifferent and ranked above all those subscripted with 2, which are in turn indifferent, there is not even a whiff of intransitivity. Since the best counter-examples to transitivity trade on such confusions, we may conclude that rational preference is transitive. (Given a large range of alternatives and required to choose between them two at a time, most subjects are unable to avoid intransitivities. But so long as they feel these as faults and are willing to straighten them out, they share the ideal that rational preference is transitive. Where there are intransitivities, there may be nothing a person *most* wants and thus he will be unable to decide rationally what to do; so it is in his interest to avoid intransitivities.)

Axiom 8D requires that i not both be indifferent between two alternatives and prefer one to the other. It might seem that when i's desires about two alternatives a and b are hopelessly conflicted, he might be said to prefer a to b and to prefer b to a. For surely i could have one good reason for preferring a to b and another but equally good reason for preferring b to a. But if that were really so and he could not choose, then (as "equally" suggests) it seems more accurate to describe the case as one in which he is indifferent between the two alternatives, rather than as one in which he prefers (on balance) either to the other. If that is more accurate, there will be two sources of indifferences: not caring one way or the other and hopeless conflict. We will then have to check whether both species of indifference persist through transitivity. Suppose i sees nothing to choose between a and b and is hopelessly conflicted between b and c. How does he feel about a and c? If he sees nothing to choose between them or is hopelessly conflicted between them, his indifference is transitive; but if he prefers one to the other, that may show him something to choose between a and b or it may resolve his conflict between *b* and *c*. Insofar as this illustrates how we straighten out our appetites, to that extent it also illustrates how committed we are to the rational ideal of transitive indifference. We may conclude that axioms 3D–9D articulate rational ideals of preference and indifference.

In order to apply axioms 12–16 to desire, we need to know how to mix alternatives. It was a leading idea of von Neumann and Morgenstern that we should mix alternatives by gambling. We may take the proportions in the closed unit interval $[0,1]$ to be probabilities. The idea is that given propositions (alternatives) x and y and given a probability $a \in [0,1]$, the mixture $m(a,x,y)$ is the proposition (alternative) that, with probability a, x, and, with probability $1 - a$, y. To illustrate this, imagine a wheel of fortune. Fix a number $a \in [0,1]$, color a of the wheel's rim red, and the rest, blue; then given alternatives x and y, $m(a,x,y)$ is the alternative that the wheel will be spun, that if the pointer winds up in the red, x, and that if it winds up in the blue, y.

Axiom 12D requires that *i* be indifferent between any alternative x and a gamble in which x is a dead cert and there is no chance of the other, whatever it might be. Axiom 13D requires that he be indifferent between, on the one hand, an a chance of x with a $1 - a$ chance of y or, on the other, a $1 - a$ chance of y with a $1 - (1 - a) = a$ chance of x. It is more than hard to think of any cases in which it would be rational for *i* to violate either.

Axiom 14D requires that *i* be indifferent between certain complex gambles and certain "reductions" of them. Let g_1 be the proposition that a fair coin is tossed, and if it comes up heads, *i* gets one dollar, but if it comes up tails, he gets nothing. g_1 is *not* offered to *i*. He is instead offered g_2, which is the proposition that a fair die is cast, and if it comes up with a one, *i* gets g_1, but if any other number comes up, *i* gets nothing. Since *i* has a chance to win something on g_2 and no chance to lose anything by it, *i* should want g_2; but how strongly? Axiom 14D requires him to want it exactly as strongly as he wants g_3, the gamble in which a fair dodeca-hedron is tossed, and if the face with a one is distinguished, i gets one dollar, but if any other face is distinguished, he gets nothing.

Lemma 18 in Appendix A of Chapter 6 articulates a con-cept of expected utility. Let g be a gamble in which with probability a, alternative x will ensue, but with probability $1 - a$, alternatively y will ensue. Lemma 18 says that the utility for i of g is a times the utility x has for him, plus $(1 - a)$ times the utility y has for him. Expected utility is often lik-ened to expected monetary value; if a is $\frac{1}{2}$, x is that i gets a dollar, and y is that i loses a dollar, then the expected mone-tary value of g is nil. The concept of expected utility should be distinguished from the principle of expected utility, that is, the principle that the rational thing to do is to maximize expected utility. Discerning a quantity in desire does not re-quire the principle of expected utility. One might say that axiom 14D should gain plausibility in proportion with the value of the concept of expected utility for various purposes but deny that the principle of expected utility is the only such purpose, or even among them.

When the consequence of an act a is not known for certain, but is known to be one of $c_1, \ldots, c_n$ with probabilities $p_1, \ldots, p_n$, then the expected utility of act a is

$$(p_1 \times u(c_1)) + \cdots + (p_n \times u(c_n))$$

where $u(c_j)$ is the utility of c_j, that is, the quantity of i's desire for c_j. The principle of expected utility for acts recommends from among the available acts those of highest expected util-ity. The principle is probably false; offered a choice between option (1), on which a coin will be tossed and, if it comes up heads, one gets $1,200,000, but if it comes up tails, one gets nothing, and option (2), an outright gift of half a million dollars, it is, as Rawls urges, sensible to prefer option (2), in order that in a choice so important (for most of us), one make the worst eventuality as good as possible; in large matters, prudence plays safe. But the upshot may be only that the expected utility of an act is not the quantity of i's desire for that act expressed in terms of the quantities of his desires for its possible consequences; it might be better to assign to a as its worst scenario the least of $u(c_1)$, . . . , $u(c_n)$, and then recommend those acts whose worst scenarios are greatest. At any rate, there is no guarantee that when an alternative is the performance of an act, the quantity of i's desire for that alternative is his expected utility for that act. But this seems compatible with using the expected utilities of gambles between extreme alternatives to put sizes to alternatives intermediate between them; and that is roughly how von Neumann and Morgenstern use expected utility. But since we are now in the overlap between psychology and ethics, we need pursue these matters no further.

It is easier to see what axiom 15D requires if we look not at it, but at lemma 5 in Appendix A of Chapter 6. Suppose that i prefers x to y and y to z. Then there should be a (unique) probability a such that i is indifferent between y and the gamble $m(a, x, z)$ between x and z. Continuity is relevant, as in 15D, because as a varies from 1 down to 0, one supposes that the attractiveness of $m(a, x, z)$ to i will vary from that of x down to that of z; so since i ranks y between x and z, one supposes that there will come a value of a at which $m(a, x, z)$ will be as attractive to i as y. Let the seductiveness of continuity principles work on you here. Consider two gambles, $m(a, x, z)$ and $m(a, y, z)$, which differ only in their first options, x and y. If i sees nothing to choose between x and y, then axiom 16D requires that he see nothing to choose between $m(a, x, z)$ and $m(a, y, z)$. One might wonder whether considering the opposition between x and z might not influence i's appetites differently from considering the opposition between y and z. But to the extent that it is hard to see how i might be rationally so influenced without his indifference between x and y being disturbed, axiom 16D is plausible.

97

The upshot is that we have a cogent enough concept of the quantity of a rational person's desire to be getting on with.

APPENDIX: ZEROS AND UNITS

To say that a quantity q's zero and unit are chosen arbitrarily is to say that $q(x) = 0$ and $q(y) = 1$ say nothing distinctive about x and y. Suppose that u is i's quantity of desire. Can we find distinctive things to say about alternatives x and y so that $u(x) = 0$ and $u(y) = 1$ will not be arbitrary?

Among the distinctive properties of the number zero is the fact that it is the additive identity, that is, that $a + 0 = a$ for any number a. Suppose we could devise a way α somehow to "add" alternatives. If there were then an alternative n such that for any alternative x, i is indifferent between x and $\alpha(x, n)$, then n would seem to be a suitably null alternative and $u(n) = 0$ would not seem arbitrary.

Since alternatives are propositions, one might wonder whether α should be conjunction, and whether, since p is logically equivalent to $p \& (qv - q)$, n could be any tautology. But conjunction is idempotent, that is, $p \& p$ is equivalent to p, whereas $2 + 2 \neq 2$; it will be useful for units that α not be idempotent. Nor do most propositions have in the sense entertained conjunctive inverses, for if p is not a tautology, then for no q is $p \& q$ a tautology; it will also be useful for units that propositions should have α inverses.

Many alternatives can be thought of as something or other happening or being the case at a certain place or at a certain time; in other words, many alternatives come with built-in dates and places. Let us pretend that the set of alternatives is the closure of a set of atomic alternatives under gambles, truth functions, and perhaps other operations. As a rough first approximation, let us also suppose that (1) every atomic alternative has a built-in, say, date; (2) for any atomic alternative p with built-in date t and any other t', there is an atomic

98

alternative that is the same as p except that its date has been shifted to t'; and (3) if p is dated t and p' is p's shift to another date t', then i is indifferent between p and p'. (It might help to secure this last to insist that t' be close to t.) Then we could experiment with the idea that to add alternatives is simply to conjoin them unless they have atoms in common, in which case the common atoms must be made to differ in date before conjunction. The idea is that when p is atomic, $\alpha(p,p)$ is the alternative under which p is repeated at different but close dates. [The point of clause (3) is that i should not care which, as it were, occurrence of p has its date shifted.] So if p is your getting some money at a certain time, $\alpha(p,p)$ is your getting twice as much over a short interval. On this idea, $pI\alpha(p,p)$ will probably fail for most p, so α will not be idempotent.

Continuing the speculation, an alternative n would be null if and only if for all alternatives p, i is indifferent between p and $\alpha(p,n)$. Note that if n and n' are both null, then

$$nI_i\alpha(n,n')I_in'$$

(assuming, as is plausible, that α commutes with respect to I), so i is indifferent between any two null alternatives, as seems desirable. For those of us who are indifferent to the details of the geology of Mars on last Tuesday, for some large number n, the proposition that there be exactly n grains of sand on Mars last Tuesday may well be null. That no proposition be null for an individual seems to require him to care with lunatic passion about everything. (If, as may not be impossible, we can find a proposition about which no sane person cares, that might be a way into beginning to calibrate different people's quantities of desire; but the real obstacles to interpersonal comparisons are the calibrations of their units.)

In a one-dimensional real vector space, a unit vector is a vector of which any other vector is a real multiple. What might it be to multiply an alternative by a real number? Suppose first that the real number a is not negative. Then a is the sum of a unique natural number k and a mantissa p, that is, a

99

real number p not less than zero but less than one. When x is an alternative and k is a natural number, let $\pi(x,k)$ be k repetitions of x; that is, $\pi(x,0)$ is a null alternative, and $\pi(x, k + 1)$ is $\alpha(\pi(x, k), x)$. Think of the mantissa p of a as a probability. Then the product $\pi(a, x)$ of a nonnegative real number $a = k + p$, where $0 \leq p < 1$, and an alternative x might be $\alpha(\rho(x, k), m(p, x, n))$, where n is null. Fix a null n. Then a positive unit would be an alternative x such that, first, xPn and, second, for any alternative y such that $yNLn$, there is a unique nonnegative real a such that $yI_i\pi(a,x)$. (If i has positive units, he will not in general be indifferent between different units.)

Taking unit vectors as a standard among various conceptions of a unit might be suggestive if one hoped that a multidimensional vector space of alternatives might be an enlightening way to accommodate at least some failures of comparability, that is, axiom 9D. The obvious way to try to begin to turn this hope into a bit more than idle speculation would be to try to detect a metric for a multidimensional vector space of alternatives, the distance between alternative vectors generalizing rank-ordering alternatives in the way that distance between points in space generalizes their lying to the left or right of one another along a straight line. But we shall pursue these speculations no further here.

We can now see that we want α inverses in order that alternatives z such that nPz shall be multiples of a unit. In a real vector space, multiplying a vector by the negative of the real number one reverses its direction from the origin. That picture suggests that we want opposites to alternatives. The opposite to a proposition *might* sometimes be its negation, but one can also think of opposition on the model of the relation between getting a dollar and losing one. At any rate, we might suppose that for each alternative x, there is an alternative $\nu(x)$ such that $\alpha(x,\nu(x))I_in$; and then we should probably suppose also that xI_iy iff $\nu(x)I_i\nu(y)$. Then, when a is negative, $\pi(a, x)$ could be $\nu(\pi(-a, x))$. It is then obvious how

100

to generalize the idea of a positive unit to a full unit; a unit is an alternative x such that, first, xPn and, second, for any alternative y, there is a unique real a such that $yI_i\pi(a,x)$. If α, n, π, ν and a unit exist (or something sufficiently like them exists), then the obscure objects of desire form a one-dimensional real vector space.

How plausible is it that there might be units? A strong form of a law of diminishing returns might claim that there are alternatives x and y such that $yPxPn$ and $yP\pi(a,x)$ for all real a. So to believe in units is to deny that returns diminish this strongly. Or if y is eternal bliss and x is getting a dollar, it might be thought that y is infinitely more desirable than x. Or if x is that i loses a dollar and y is that the Nazis torture i's mother to death slowly, then the claim that there is an a such that $yI_i\pi(a,x)$ sounds either like a piece of cynicism or a slander against poor i. We might get some way toward handling this last difficulty if i's ethics and his prudence were different dimensions of i's motivational space; but to do that seriously, we would want to discern how to rotate an advantage into a virtue.

8

Belief

Can what von Neumann and Morgenstern did for the quantity of desire be done for the quantity of belief? We shall argue that it can indeed be done, but before doing so, let us circumnavigate a blind alley.

It might seem the course of least effort that just as one might purloin von Neumann and Morgenstern's utility as a quantity of desire, so also sloth would suggest appropriating Leonard J. Savage's subjective probability as a quantity of belief. This strategy is a mistake.

Savage's work on subjective probability is among the very best;[1] but it was never intended for use in a defense of dualism, and certain features make it less than ideal for that purpose. In the first place, subjective probability is intended to be at least a variety of probability. But although we want a quantity of belief, it is not obvious that it must be some sort of probability. The point may emerge a bit more clearly if one thinks about zeros and units. The Kolmogoroff axioms require that probability be normalized, that is, that there be something, assigned probability 1, than which nothing is more probable, and something, assigned probability 0, than which nothing is less probable. Though it is not implausible that tautologies and contradictions have these properties, the prominence probability gives to such units and zeros makes subjective probability at least feel like a quantity of a sort different from that of utility. So even if those zeros and units are there for the taking, it would be pleasant not to have to highlight them.

The second matter goes a bit deeper. In Savage's theory, we

begin with a set S of states and a set F of consequences. The set of acts, A, is the set of functions from S to F, and preference and indifference are, in the first instance, relations between acts. Events are subsets of S, and subjective probability is defined on events. So although Savage demonstrates the existence of both a unique subjective probability and a utility unique up to a positive linear transformation, these two are, in the first instance, functions with different domains.

For our purposes, this approach has two unattractive features. First, for reasons that will emerge, it would be good to maximize the chances that there are lawful relations between different psychological quantities. It is harder to envisage lawful relations between quantities with different domains than between quantities with the same domain; one does not expect interesting laws to connect the masses of stones with the number of prime divisions of an integer. We should thus like our psychological quantities to have the same domain. This is not to suggest that Savage could not engineer from his utility and subjective probability quantities with the same domain; but because the straightforward is more persuasive *ceteris paribus* in philosophy than the clever, we should avoid ingenuity. Moreover, and this introduces the second feature, they should nonetheless be genuinely different quantities. One does not expect interesting laws (except perhaps mathematical ones) to connect the masses of stones with their doubles; but both masses and velocities are quantities had by stones, and partly because they are different, but more because there are lawful relations between them (involving forces, of course), mechanics is worth doing. Partly because Savage treats utility and subjective probability together, and more because Savage analyzes a person's believing that one event is at least as probable as another in terms of his preferences and indifferences between certain special acts, one might come to wonder whether his subjective probability and utility are, in the requisite sense, genuinely different quantities. (None of these remarks is a serious criticism of Savage.)

103

It is at this point that formalizing a general account of quantity, as we did above, may pay off. Suppose that for each individual i, there are binary relations between propositions that are to i's belief as his preference and indifference are to his desire, that is, that satisfy the corresponding axioms 1B–16B. Then, at a stroke, the general account will yield a quantity of belief with the same domain as the quantity of desire; but at the same time, if we can argue that the relations underlying the quantity of belief can vary independently of the relations underlying the quantity of desire, these two quantities will be genuinely different, that is, different enough that, for all we know, there might be genuinely lawful relations between them.

That much understood, it seems obvious enough how we might begin. For each individual i, let S_i be the binary propositional attitude that relates an alternative p to an alternative q if and only if i is surer that p than that q; and let T_i be the binary propositional attitude that holds if and only if i is as sure that p as that q. The relevant notion is one of rational belief, and it is as normative as was our earlier notion of rational desire. The variety of rational belief we have in mind here requires neither much good evidence on which belief should be based nor much in the way of sound reasoning; no more did our earlier conception of rational desire require an absence of neurosis. All either requires is a wholly internal and broadly structural sort of rationality, the structure being that specified by axioms 1–16. In both cases, we may think of rationality as a theoretical simplification or idealization akin to rigidity or the absence of friction in elementary mechanics.

Axiom 9B requires that when i is surer of neither of two alternatives than of the other, he is equally (which may be very little) sure of both. Some such principle seems to be connected with our thinking heads as likely as tails or, of dice, that a six is as likely as a four; in the absence of a reason for thinking one more likely than the other, we think neither more likely than the other and *thus* think them equally likely. As with desire, there may indeed be genuine failures of comparability here; but the will to know, curiosity, urges us against the modesty of ignorance toward comparison. It is in the interest of a curious person that he compare relevant hypotheses in order to organize his investigations efficiently. If there are genuine failures of comparability, then for all we know a multidimensional space of alternatives, like that entertained in passing in the appendix of Chapter 7, might suggest ways to deal with them.

Axiom 3B requires that i be as sure that p as that p; it is hard to see how he might fail to be. Axiom 4B says that if i is as sure that p as that q, then he is as sure that q as that p; symmetry seems almost as much built into the grammar here as it was into that of indifference. One has a moral certainty that ingenuity can devise long sequences of propositions in which one is as certain of each as of its immediate successor but in which one is vastly more sure of the first than of the last. Indeed, the famous sorites arguments, like the paradoxes of the bald man and of the heap, would seem clearly to fit this description. But with all due respect to Peter Unger[2] (and the respect due a man of his intellectual courage is immense), the fact that we find these sorites paradoxical suggests that we think something is wrong with them somewhere. There are waters too deep to venture over here; the problem of saying *exactly* what *vagueness* is seems to be very difficult indeed. Nonetheless, it seems, these considerations indicate that we feel a push toward satisfying axiom 5B.

Axiom 6B requires that i not be surer that p than that p, and this seems sensible enough. Axiom 7B requires that being surer than be transitive; here is what purports to be a counterexample (formally similar to the scissors–paper–stone example of the previous chapter). Suppose there are before us four cubes, A, B, C, and D, on whose faces numerals are inscribed thus:

A	B	C	D
0	3	2	5
4 0 4	3 3 3	2 2 2	1 1 1
4	3	6	5
4	3	6	5

P and Q are each to pick one cube apiece, one of them before the other. They will then play a (long series of) game(s) in which each will roll his respective cube; whoever's uppermost number is lower will pay the other one dollar. Note that (a) A beats B in $4 \times 6 = 24$ cases and loses in the other 12, so A beats B by a margin of 2 to 1; (b) B beats C in $6 \times 4 = 24$ cases and loses in the other $6 \times 2 = 12$, so B beats C by a margin of 2 to 1; (c) C beats D in $(4 \times 3) + (2 \times 6) = 24$ cases and loses in the other $4 \times 3 = 12$ cases, so C beats D by a margin of 2 to 1; and (d) D beats A in $(3 \times 6) + (3 \times 2) = 24$ cases and loses in the other $4 \times 3 = 12$ cases, so D beats A by a margin of 2 to 1. Hence, no matter which cube the first of them to pick might take, the other can pick a cube that beats it by a margin of 2 to 1.

The fact that whoever picks second has a good strategy does not evince an intransitivity. It seems no less confused to believe that there is a rational intransitivity of preference in this example than in the earlier scissors–paper–stone example. But one might think that (1) A is more likely to win than B; (2) B is more likely to win than C; (3) C is more likely to win than D; and (4) D is more likely to win than A. Surely, the objection goes, there is an intransitivity in (1)–(4). Perhaps, but it is a scope confusion to think it an intransitivity in the "surer than" relation. The objector seems to be supposing that the relevant propositions are

x: A wins, y: B wins,
z: C wins, w: D wins,

and that i has good reason to be surer that x than that y, that y than that z, that z than that w, and that w than that x; were i's beliefs like that, there would be an intransitivity in his "surer than" relation. But i cannot be surer that A wins, no matter what his opponent plays, than that B wins, no matter what his opponent plays. As before, the alternatives have been misleadingly specified; the objection trades on confusing being surer of one subject–predicate proposition than another with being surer of one relation proposition than another. Consider these more prolix propositions:

x_1: A beats B, y_1: B beats C,
x_2: B beats A, y_2: C beats B,
z_1: C beats D, w_1: D beats A,
z_2: D beats C, w_2: A beats D.

Here i has good reason to be surer that x_1 than x_2, that y_1 than y_2, that z_1 than z_2, and that w_1 than w_2. But there would be an intransitivity in this (of the sort the objector seems to be supposing) only if i also had reason to be surer that x_2 than y_1, that y_2 than z_1, that z_2 than w_1, and that w_2 than x_1. However, the example makes it clear that this is not so; i ought to be as sure of any one of x_1, y_1, z_1, w_1 as any other, be surer of each than any one of x_2, y_2, z_2, w_2, and be as sure of any two of these. The structure here is exactly that of the scissors–paper–stone example, and no more exhibits an intransitivity in the being-surer-than relation than that earlier example revealed one in preference. Granted the truth, or high likelihood, of x_1, y_1, z_1, and w_1, there will be an intransitivity in the beating relation, or the likelihood-of-beating relation. But we have never allowed ourselves to detect that much structure *inside* the propositions that are our alternatives; so such intransitivities do not seem to be a special difficulty for

107

detecting a quantity of belief, as opposed to devising games or, *perhaps*, probability (which need not be subjective). Since this seems to be the most interesting putative counterexample to the transitivity of being rationally surer than, we may conclude that this relation is transitive.[3]

Axiom 8B requires that *i* not be both surer of one alternative than another and as sure of one as the other. It is a familiar fact of intellectual life that evidence can be conflicting, that is, that some evidence may favor one hypothesis over a second, whereas the rest of the evidence may support the second more than the first. If the balance is unequal, *i* ought rationally to be surer of the better supported hypothesis; but if genuinely equal balance occurs, *i* ought rationally to be as sure (however little) of the one hypothesis as of the other. If so, we may have two sorts of equality, deadlocked but opposed lines of thought and the absence of anything to decide between alternatives. Thus, when *i* is deadlocked between *p* and *q* but sees nothing to decide between *q* and *r*, axiom 5B requires that he be as sure that *p* as that *r*; but should he be surer of one of *p* and *r* than the other, 5B will still hold if the imbalance between *p* and *r* either breaks the deadlock between *p* and *q* or decides *i* between *q* and *r*. The urge thus to straighten out our convictions illustrates how axioms 1B–9B articulate norms of rational belief.

In order to evaluate axioms 12B–16B, we need an interpretation of mixing suitable for comparative conviction. In order to motivate (rather than justify) a suitable interpretation of mixing, it is easiest to reason backward from the main result we want about mixtures, namely, linearity. What we want is a quantity *q* of belief, and we want it to be linear on mixtures, that is, we want it to turn out that

$$q(m(a, x, y)) = aq(x) + (1 - a)q(y)$$

where *a* is any probability and *x* and *y* are any alternatives. Let us try to solve, as it were, this equation for *m*; to do so, concentrate on its right-hand side. Let us pretend that we

108

already have q, and let us think of q as assigning probabilities to alternatives. Then, in the large, the right-hand side is a sum of probabilities. The probability of the disjunction of two mutually exclusive alternatives is the sum of their separate probabilities, so it would be pleasant if we could ensure that the two terms of the sum be the probabilities of each of two mutually exclusive alternatives. Each of these terms is the product of a probability and what we are thinking of as another probability. The probability of the conjunction of two independent alternatives is the product of their separate probabilities, so it would be pleasant if we could ensure that each of the two products be the probability of the conjunction of two independent alternatives. These reflections about mutual exclusivity and independence give us the principle items in terms of which we may solve for m. To make the solution vivid, imagine an omniscient and honorable but taciturn being; let us call her the Pythoness. Given a probability a and alternatives x and y, the Pythoness will make a fair wheel of fortune whose workings are completely independent of x and y and, in particular, of any other wheels of fortune already "mentioned" in x or y. She then colors a of the wheel's rim red, and the rest (that is, $1 - a$) blue. The plan is that she will then spin the wheel, and if either the needle lands in the red and x or the needle lands in the blue and y, she will do something distinctive, like stand on her head; but she will refrain from doing so if neither. However, i must make his judgments *before* she spins the wheel. That is, for any alternative z, $m(a, x, y) S_i z$ if and only if before she spins the wheel, i is surer that she will stand on her head than that z; $m(a, x, y) T_i z$ if and only if before the spin, i is as sure that she will stand on her head as that z; and $z S_i m(a, x, y)$ if and only if before the spin, i is surer that z than that she will stand on her head. If we really did have q already, then m could be said clearly to fill the middle positions of q, and then the satisfaction of axioms 12B–16B would be automatic. But since we were only pretending to have q, we must now check to see whether m does indeed satisfy 12B–16B, that is, whether those axioms are true on the interpretation of m that we now intend.

Axiom 12B requires that i be as sure that x as that she will stand on her head when all of the wheel's rim is red and none of it blue. Axiom 13B asks i to consider two gambles. In the first, a of its wheel is red, the rest, or $1 - a$ of it, is blue, and she will stand on her head if and only if either x and red comes up or y and blue comes up. In the second, $1 - a$ of its wheel is red, the rest, or $1 - (1 - a) = a$ of it, is blue, and she will stand on her head if and only if either y and red comes up or x and blue comes up. Axiom 13B requires that i be as sure that she will stand on her head in the first gamble as that she will stand on her head in the second. Both axioms do no more than articulate features of our interpretation of mixing.

Axiom 14B requires that i be as sure of the outcome of certain complex or nested gambles as of their "reductions." It may be easier to see what 14B requires if we replace wheels of fortune with other devices. Suppose that under gamble g_1, a fair coin will be tossed; the Pythoness will yodel if and only if either x and heads comes up or y and tails comes up. Do not ask i how sure he is about whether she will yodel. Do ask him to consider gamble g_2 under which a fair die will be cast; the Pythoness will stand on her head if and only if either a four comes up and she yodels under g_1 or y and any other number comes up. Ask him also to consider gamble g_3 under which a fair dodecahedron will be tossed; she will compute the value of e to sixteen places if and only if either x and the face with a 9 is distinguished or y and any other face is distinguished. Axion 14B requires that i be as sure that she will stand on her head under g_2 as that she will compute the value of e to sixteen places under g_3.

Axiom 14B requires that i's expectations accord with one of the least controversial principles of probability, that illustrated by reducing a coin toss plus rolling a die to casting a dodecahedron. The arithmetic is that stated explicitly in ax-

110

iom 14. *If* we wanted a quantity of belief in order to found subjective probability *and* we thought subjective probability were the only sort of probability, there might be more than a whiff of vicious circularity in supposing *i*'s convictions to accord with probability calculations in order to found a quantity of belief. But we are not aiming at founding subjective probability, and we shall never need to claim that subjective probability is the only real probability; so there is no circularity in supposing *i* astute enough to form his convictions in accordance with the requirements of 14B (which does not mean that he must think in our terms or calculate). That understood, 14B seems reasonable enough.

It is again easier to see what axiom 15B requires if we look not at it, but at lemma 5 in Appendix A of Chapter 6. Suppose that *i* is surer that x than that y and surer that y than that z. Then there should be a unique probability a such that given that the Pythoness will snap her fingers if and only if either x and red, which colors a of the wheel, comes up or z and blue, which colors the rest, comes up, *i* is as sure that she will snap her fingers as that y. Continuity, as in 15B, is relevant because as a varies from one down to zero, one supposes that *i*'s conviction that she will snap her fingers under $m(a, x, z)$ will vary from his degree of conviction that x down to his degree of conviction that z; so since *i* ranks y between x and z, one supposes that there will come a value of a at which *i* will be as sure that she will snap her fingers under $m(a, x, z)$ as that y. Let the ancient and honorable principle that nature makes no leaps work on you here.

Consider two gambles, $m(a, x, z)$ and $m(a, y, z)$, which differ only in their first alternatives, x and y. Under the first, the Pythoness will stand on her head if and only if either x and red, which colors a of the wheel, comes up or z and blue, which colors the rest, comes up. Under the second, she will wiggle her ears if and only if either y and red, which again colors a of the wheel, comes up or z and blue, which again colors the rest, comes up. Suppose *i* is as sure that x as that y.

111

Axiom 16B requires that i be as sure that she will stand on her head under $m(a, x, z)$ as that she will wiggle her ears under $m(a, y, z)$. If one wonders whether considering z with x might not influence i's conviction differently from considering z with y, then if one also notices that this ought rationally not to happen without altering his standoff between x and y, then one ought to find 16B plausible. Hence, it would seem, axioms 12B–16B are true under our present interpretation of mixing alternatives. Therefore, there is a quantity of belief that is unique except for the choice of its zero point and unit length and that has the same domain of alternatives as our quantity of desire. (Or rather their domains coincide to the extent that it is reasonable to suppose that i can make appetitive comparisons between all and only those alternatives between which he can make sureness comparisons.)

There remains the question of the independence of these two quantities, and here it would only be natural to be curious about Savage's analysis of being surer in terms of preference. Savage's idea is compelling. Suppose, first, that there are two circumstances, call them p for profit and l for loss, and that i prefers p to l. Consider next two propositions, q and r; we want to know whether i is surer that q than that r, or not. We imagine two acts, a_q and a_r, with the following properties: a_q will result in profit p if q, but in loss l otherwise; and similarly, a_r will result in profit p if r, but in loss l otherwise. Then Savage's idea is that i is surer that q than that r if and only if he prefers (someone performing) a_q to (someone performing) a_r; for he will prefer that act whose performance he is more confident will yield the result he prefers. Waiving, as we ought, niggling doubts about profits and losses too small for i to take the choice between a_q and a_r seriously, it cannot be denied that Savage's idea is attractive. (Savage says that the idea was suggested to him by a passage in the writings of Bruno de Finetti.)

The sort of independence between belief and desire that we want is in no way incompatible with the correctness of Savage's analysis. For what Savage has noticed is that whether i is surer that q than that r is not independent of a very special preference, namely, whether i prefers act a_q to act a_r. But the existence of this dependency is compatible with the absence of a dependency between whether i is surer that q than that r and whether i prefers q to r; and it is this last independence that we want. Note that none of our axioms about desire says anything about belief, and none of our axioms about belief says anything about desire. To secure identity of domains, it would suffice to assume that xP_iy or xI_iy or yP_ix if and only if xS_iy or xT_iy or yS_ix; no disjunct on one side is linked to a disjunct on the other.

What we want is that for at least some alternatives, nine sorts of co-occurrence should be possible. For example, it should be possible that i prefers q to r, but is also surer that q than that r, or is also as sure that q as that r, or is also surer that r than that q; and it should be possible that i is surer that q than that r, but also prefers q to r, or is also indifferent between q and r, or also prefers r to q; and so on through all nine pairs whose first member is one of three things and whose second member is one of three other things. It seems a fact of life that all nine combinations occur, so we shall assume what we might call the static or instantaneous version of the independence we want. But its dynamic version seems no less plain. Suppose the menu at your local restaurant varies mysteriously, but that you are, say, as sure that they will have leeks on the menu on Tuesday (when you usually go there) as that they will then have tomatoes on the menu. It seems perfectly possible that you might begin by preferring leeks to tomatoes but that as you grow tired of leeks, you first come to be indifferent between them and tomatoes, and then come to prefer tomatoes to leeks. None of this seems to require any change in your convictions about what will be on the menu on Tuesday, nor that they be equal rather than weighted toward one side. Conversely, it seems no less possible that your taste, whatever it might be, in vegetables remain fixed

113

while your comparative confidence about Tuesday's menu vary from being weighted toward tomatoes through equality to being weighted toward leeks. If all this seems like laboring the obvious, then at least we agree that the quantities of belief and desire are (conceptually) independent quantities; but we labor what should be obvious because some fashionable psychological holisms sometimes seem to blind theorists to the obvious.

We may conclude that for each person i, there are quantities of i's desire and his belief that are both unique except (perhaps) for the choice of their zero points and unit lengths, which have the same domains of alternatives or propositions and which are conceptually independent enough that, for all we know, there might be genuinely lawful relations between them.

APPENDIX: CONVICTION AND PROBABILITY

There are infinitely many functions from the set A of propositions to the set of real numbers that encode the individual i's conviction; is one of them i's subjective probability? We cannot settle this question unless we can recognize probability. Let us follow custom and agree that probability satisfies the Kolmogoroff axioms (excluding, perhaps, countable additivity). Even if these axioms do not suffice to individuate probability, we may nevertheless ask whether one of the quantities of i's conviction satisfies them. This question requires in turn that A be closed under something like unions and complements, or disjunction and negation. Set A would satisfy this requirement if it were a Boolean algebra.

In order that A be a Boolean algebra, it needs first a partial order. Assume, then, that there is a binary relation $\geq$ on A that is reflexive,

$$x \geq x,$$

antisymmetric,

114

$$(x \geq y \ \& \ y \geq x) \rightarrow x = y,$$

and transitive,

$$(x \geq y \ \& \ y \geq z) \rightarrow x \geq z.$$

Next we need meets and joins. Assume that there are two binary functions, $\vee$ and $\wedge$, on A. For the meet, $x \wedge y$, of x and y, assume that

$$x \geq x \wedge y, \quad y \geq x \wedge y, \quad (x \geq z \ \& \ y \geq z) \rightarrow x \wedge y \geq z,$$

and for their join, $x \vee y$, that

$$x \vee y \geq x, \quad x \vee y \geq y, \quad (z \geq x \ \& \ z \geq y) \rightarrow z \geq x \vee y.$$

A top in A is a member of x of A such that $x \geq y$ for all y in A, and a floor in A is a member of x of A such that $y \geq x$ for all y in A; assume that A has a top t and a floor f. A member y of A is a complement of a member x of A if and only if $x \vee y = t$ and $x \wedge y = f$. Assume the distributive laws,

$$(x \vee y) \wedge z = (x \wedge z) \vee (y \wedge z),$$
$$(x \wedge y) \vee z = (x \vee z) \wedge (y \vee z),$$

and that each member of A has a complement. Then x has a unique complement, which is known as $\bar{x}$. A is now a Boolean algebra.

Write xR_iy for xS_iy or xT_iy. Assume that tR_ix and xR_if for all x and that tS_if. Among the quantities encoding i's conviction, there is a unique q, which is normalized in the sense that $q(t) = 1$ and $q(f) = 0$. Consider the following:

(a) $$q(\bar{x}) = 1 - q(x),$$
(b) $$x \wedge y = f \rightarrow q(x \vee y) = q(x) + q(y).$$

Since q is normalized, (a) and (b) seem to be reasonable reconstructions of the other Kolmogoroff axioms (excluding countable additivity). (When probability is defined on "parts" of a large "space" like t, it is not in general possible for it to be both countably additive and defined on all parts; so since q is total, we should forgo countable additivity.) Have we by now assumed enough to be able to prove (a) and (b)?

The answer is no. Let A be the set of all Lebesgue measurable subsets of the unit square and let μ be Lebesgue measure on A. If you are not familiar with measure theory, you may think of A as a Boolean algebra including all the polygons in the unit square and of μ as area. For each x in A, let $q(x)$ be the nonnegative square root of $2\mu(x) - (\mu(x))^2$. [If the range of μ on A is thought of as the unit interval on the x axis, then q takes its members to the ordinates of the points on the quarter arc of the unit circle centered at $(1, 0)$ and lying in the unit square.] For x and y in A, say that xS_iy if and only if $q(x) > q(y)$, and xT_iy iff $q(x) = q(y)$. For any a in $[0, 1]$ and any x and y in A, let $c(a, x, y)$ be $aq(x) + (1 - a)q(y)$. Since $c(a, x, y)$ is in $[0, 1]$, so is $(c(a, x, y))^2$, and thus $1 - (c(a, x, y))^2$ is also in $[0, 1]$. Let r be its nonnegative square root; since r is in $[0, 1]$, so is $1 - r$. Then for any z in A such that $\mu(z) = 1 - r$, we may let $m(a, x, y)$ be z; z could be any square with side the nonnegative square root of $1 - r$, and there are such squares in A. Then $q(z) = aq(x) + (1 - a)q(y)$, so A fills the middle positions of q. Thus, S_i, T_i, and m satisfy the axioms of the preceding chapter. So since A is also a Boolean algebra under the usual set-theoretic operations and relations, and since q is normalized, we have a model for all that we have assumed so far.

But theses (a) and (b) both fail in this model. In the figure, let x be triangle $AB0$ and let y be triangle $CB0$; then $x \vee y$ is square $ABC0$. $\mu(x \vee y) = \frac{1}{4}$, so $q(x \vee y)$ is $\sqrt{7}/4$. $\mu(x) =$

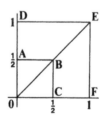

$\mu(y) = \frac{1}{8}$, so $q(x) = q(y) = \sqrt{15}/8$. Hence, $q(x \vee y) = \sqrt{7}/4 < \sqrt{15}/4 = q(x) + q(y)$, although $x \wedge y = f$; hence, (b) fails. Now let x be triangle $DE0$; $\bar{x}$ is triangle $EF0$. $\mu(x) = \mu(\bar{x}) = \frac{1}{2}$, so $q(x) = q(\bar{x}) = \sqrt{3}/4$, so $q(x) + q(\bar{x}) = \sqrt{3}/2 < 1$; hence, (a) fails. [By centering our circle at $(0, 1)$, rather than at $(1, 0)$, we could have reversed both inequalities.] Hence, the unique normalized quantity of a person's convictions in a Boolean algebra of propositions cannot be proved to satisfy (a) and (b). So if satisfaction of (a) and (b) is necessary for any sort of probability, and thus for subjective probability, the unique normalized quantity of a person's convictions cannot be proved to be his subjective probabil

Given normalization, (a) follows from (b); for $x \wedge \bar{x} = f$, so by (b), $q(x) + q(\bar{x}) = q(x \vee \bar{x}) = q(t) = 1$. Hence, in order that q satisfy (a) and (b), it is necessary and sufficient that

(c)   if $x T_i m(a, t, f)$, $y T_i m(b, t, f)$, and $x \wedge y = f$, then $a + b \leq 1$ [so $m(a + b, t, f)$ exists] and $m(a + b, t, f) T_i x \vee y$.

First we derive (b) from (c). Suppose that $x \wedge y = f$. There are unique $a, b \in [0, 1]$ such that $x T_i m(a, t, f)$ and $y T_i m(b, t, f)$; $q(x) = a$ and $q(y) = b$. Since $x \wedge y = f$, by (c) $a + b \leq 1$, so $m(a + b, t, f)$ exists and $x \vee y T_i m(a + b, t, f)$. Thus, $q(x \vee y) = q(m(a + b, t, f)) = a + b = q(x) + q(y)$. Next we derive (c) from (b). Suppose that $x T_i m(a, t, f)$, $y T_i m(b, t, f)$, and $x \wedge y = f$. Since $x \vee y \in A$, $q(x \vee y) \leq 1$, and since $q(x) = a$, $q(y) = b$, and by (b), $q(x \vee y) = q(x) + q(y)$, $a + b \leq 1$. Moreover,

$$
\begin{aligned}
q(x \vee y) &= q(m(q(x \vee y), t, f)) \\
&= q(m(q(x) + q(y), t, f)) \\
&= q(m(a + b, t, f)),
\end{aligned}
$$

so $m(a + b, t, f) T_i x \vee y$. Hence, (c) states an independent connection between the quantitative structure that S_i, T_i, and m impose on A and its Boolean algebra that is necessary and sufficient for i's unique normalized quantity of belief to satisfy (a) and (b), the other two Kolmogoroff axioms of probability. Thesis (c) articulates exactly what there is to a person's

117

subjective probability that is not a logical consequence of his having normalized degrees of belief in the members of a Boolean algebra of propositions.

What (c) requires can be illustrated as follows. Let x and y be propositions, let i be a person, and let a and b be members of $[0, 1]$. Build three wheels of fortune, 1, 2, and 3. Color a of 1's rim red, and the rest, green; color b of 2's rim orange, and the rest, blue. If $a + b < 1$, color $a + b$ of 3's rim yellow, and the rest, violet; otherwise, color all of 3's rim yellow. Suppose i is as sure that x as that 1 will come up red and as sure that y as that 2 will come up orange. Let z be i's paradigm contradiction; z might, for example, be the proposition that $2^{157} + 1$ both is and is not prime. Then (c) requires that i not be surer that x or y than that 3 will come up yellow, and that if i is surer that 3 will come up yellow than that x or y, then i is surer that x and y than that z.

Nevertheless, principle (c) is conceptually so close to (b) that their derivations from one another provide very little insight into either. Perhaps there is a scheme of several distinct connections between, on the one hand, the quantitative structure that S_i, T_i, and m impose on A and, on the other, its Boolean algebra, such that, given normalization, this scheme conjointly suffices for (b), but its separate links are individually more perspicuous than, or conceptually further removed from (b) than, (c). Such a scheme might provide some more insight into (b). The following is a scheme of connections that suffices for (b):

(d) $$x \geq y \rightarrow x R_i y,$$

(e) $$(x \geq y \ \& \ x \geq z \ \& \ y T_i z) \rightarrow x \wedge \bar{y} T_i x \wedge \bar{z},$$

(f) $$x \vee y \geq m(a, x, y),$$

(g) $$x \wedge \overline{m(a, x, f)} \, T_i m(1 - a, x, f).$$

Granted (d)–(g), we can first derive a lemma:

Lemma. $q(x) = q(x \wedge y) + q(x \wedge \bar{y})$.

118

Proof. Since $x \geq x \wedge y$, $x R_i x \wedge y$ by (d), so for some $a \in [0, 1]$, $x \wedge y T_i m(a, x, f)$. By (f), $x \geq m(a, x, f)$, so since $x \wedge \bar{y} = x \wedge \overline{(x \wedge y)}$,

$$x \wedge \bar{y} \, T_i x \wedge \overline{(x \wedge y)} \, T_i x \wedge \overline{m(a, x, f)} \, T_i m(1 - a, x, f)$$

by (e) and (g). Thus,

$$q(x \wedge y) + q(x \wedge \bar{y}) = a q(x) + (1 - a) q(x) = q(x). \quad \blacksquare$$

It is a corollary of this lemma that

$$q(x \vee y) = q(x \wedge \bar{y}) + q(x \wedge y) + q(y \wedge \bar{x}).$$

Thesis (b) follows from the corollary; for if $x \wedge y = f$, $x \wedge \bar{y} = x$, and $y \wedge \bar{x} = y$, so

$$\begin{aligned} q(x \vee y) &= q(x \wedge \bar{y}) + q(x \wedge y) + q(y \wedge \bar{x}) \\ &= q(x) + 0 + q(y) \\ &= q(x) + q(y). \end{aligned}$$

It also follows from the corollary that

$$\begin{aligned} q(x \vee y) &= (q(x \wedge \bar{y}) + q(x \wedge y) + q(y \wedge \bar{x})) \\ &\quad + (q(x \wedge y) - q(x \wedge y)) \\ &= (q(x \wedge \bar{y}) + q(x \wedge y)) + (q(y \wedge x) \\ &\quad + q(y \wedge \bar{x})) - q(x \wedge y) \\ &= q(x) + q(y) - q(x \wedge y). \end{aligned}$$

If we think of $q(x) + q(y)$ as "counting" $x \wedge y$ twice, we could call this result a principle of double counting; it is reminiscent of the pigeonhole principle in algebra, and it entails that if $q(x) + q(y) > q(x \vee y)$, then $x \wedge y S_i f$. Thesis (a) is the case of the lemma in which x is t.

In the present context (that is, the assumptions about S_i, T_i, and m made in the preceding chapter, A's Boolean algebra, and normalization), (b) therefore follows from (d)–(g). The converse is not quite true. Given (b), (d) follows; for if $x \geq y$, $x = y \vee (x \wedge \bar{y})$, where $y \wedge (x \wedge \bar{y}) = f$, so $q(x) = q(y) + q(x \wedge \bar{y}) \geq q(y)$, and thus $x R_i y$. Given (b), (e) also follows; for if $x \geq y$ and $x \geq z$, $q(y) + q(x \wedge \bar{y}) = q(x) = q(z) + q(x \wedge \bar{z})$ as before, and if $y\,T_i z$, $q(y) = q(z)$, so $q(x \wedge \bar{y}) = q(x \wedge \bar{z})$, so $x \wedge \bar{y}\,T_i x \wedge \bar{z}$. Moreover, given (b) *and* (f), (g) follows; for given (f), $x \geq m(a,x,f)$, so given (b)

$$q(x) = q(m(a,x,f) + q(x \wedge \overline{m(a,x,f)})).$$

Thus,

$$
\begin{aligned}
q(x \wedge \overline{m(a,x,f)})) &= q(x) - aq(x) \\
&= (1 - a)q(x) \\
&= q(m(1 - a, x, f)),
\end{aligned}
$$

so $x \wedge \overline{m(a,x,f)}\,T_i m(1 - a, x, f)$. But even in the present context, (f) does not follow from (b). Once again let A be the set of all Lebesgue measurable subsets of the unit square, but now let q be Lesbesgue measure on A. Set A is a Boolean algebra under the usual set-theoretic operations and relations, and q is both normalized and additive. For $x, y \in A$, say that $x S_i y$ iff $q(x) > q(y)$, and $x T_i y$ iff $q(x) = q(y)$. For any $x, y \in A$ and any $a \in [0, 1]$, let r be the nonnegative square root of $aq(x) + (1 - a)q(y)$ and let z be the square with vertices at $(0,0)$, $(0, r)$, (r, r), and $(r, 0)$. Then $q(z) = aq(x) + (1 - a)q(y)$, so A fills the middle positions of q; thus, if we set $m(a, x, y) = z$, then S_i, T_i, and m satisfy the axioms of the preceding chapter. Let x be the square with vertices at $(1, 1)$, $(1, .9)$, $(.9, .9)$, and $(.9, 1)$, and let y be the square with vertices at $(.9, 1)$, $(.9, .9)$, $(.8, .9)$, and $(.8, 1)$. Then for any a, $m(a, x, y)$ is the square with vertices at $(0,0)$, $(.1, 0)$, $(.1, .1)$, and $(0, .1)$. Hence, $m(a, x, y)$ is disjoint from $x \vee y$, not a subset of it. So although (d)–(g) are sufficient for (b) in the present context, they are a bit more than an analysis of it.

The gap is (f). Let x and y be propositions and let a be any member of $[0, 1]$. Build a fair wheel of fortune whose action is independent of whether x or not and of whether y or not; color a of its rim vermilion, and the rest, ultramarine. In Chapter 8, we understood $m(a, x, y)$ as the proposition that x and vermillion will come up, or else y and ultramarine will come up. Interpreting Boolean algebra by propositional calculus, $x \vee y$ is the disjunction of x and y. If neither x nor y, then it is not true that x and vermilion will come up, and it is not true that y and ultramarine will come up; so $x \vee y$ is a consequence of $m(a, x, y)$. Hence, (f) is true under its intended interpretation. So we have independent grounds for (f); and adding (f) to the present context, (b) is equivalent to (d), (e), and (g).

What do (d), (e), and (g) mean? Thesis (d) does not mean that i believes all logical consequences of his beliefs. But it does require him not to be surer of a belief of his than of any of its (at least truth functional) consequences; so i should not be confident of his beliefs that have implausible (truth functional) consequences. This seems an ideal of belief, granted the counsel of perfection that we should consider all of a proposition's consequences when making up our minds about that proposition. Thus, (d) coheres with our normative understanding of rational belief.

Theses (e) and (g) account for the arithmetic in (b). Taken physically, in terms of area, (e) and (g) are overwhelming. Thesis (e) is a principle of subtraction: if x is a region with parts y and z of the same area as each other, then x with y cut out has the same area as x with z cut out. Given (f), (g) says that x with its a-part cut out has the same area as the $(1 - a)$-part of x. (It does not matter *which* a-part of x we take as *the* a-part of x.) Probability and area have a good deal in common; it may be that credence leaks from a physical understanding of the Kolmogoroff axioms into their probabilistic interpretation.

On the intended interpretation, (e) requires that if i is as sure that y as that z, and if x is a consequence of y and z, then i is as sure that x but not y as that x but not z. The constraint that x be a consequence of each is not vacuous. Let d be a fair die, let x be the proposition that d will come up even (2, 4, or 6), let y be the proposition that d will come up 4, and let w be the proposition that d will come up 5. It is sensible for i to be as sure that y as that w. x is not a consequence of w, and $x \wedge \bar{w}$

121

is equivalent to x; but x is a consequence of y, and i should be surer that x than that $x \wedge \bar{y}$; i should not be as sure that $x \wedge \bar{w}$ (even) as that $x \wedge \bar{y}$ (2 or 6). But if z is the proposition that d will come up 2, then i should be as sure that y as that z, x is a consequence of y and of z, and i should be as sure that $x \wedge \bar{y}$ (2 or 6) as that $x \wedge \bar{z}$ (4 or 6). We mentioned in connection with (d) the counsel of perfection that we should consider all of a proposition's consequences when making up our minds about that proposition. The point of (g) is that, in order to compare y with z, considering a consequence x of y and of z should include comparing $x \wedge \bar{y}$ with $x \wedge \bar{z}$. Granted the counsel of perfection, this point coheres with our normative conception of belief.

As for (g), let x be a proposition and pick a from $[0, 1]$. Build a fair wheel of fortune whose action is independent of whether x or not; color a of its rim red, and the rest blue. Let y be the proposition that x and the wheel will come up red, and let z be the proposition that x and the wheel will come up blue. [It is in the nature of (g) that it allows us to economize on wheels.] Then (g) requires i to be as sure that x but not y as that z. Why should not intuition have a finite velocity? If i is given a moment to think he can see that

x but not y if and only if x but the wheel does not come up red,
if and only if x and the wheel comes up blue,
if and only if z.

Since i can thus be certain that x but not y if and only if z, he can be as sure that x but not y, as that z. Thus, (g) is true under its intended interpretation. (The inference from being certain that x if and only if y to being as sure that x as that y deserves comment. Being sure that x if and only if y is not the same as being as sure that x as that y; the first is the application of a unary propositional attitude to a biconditional, whereas the second is a binary propositional attitude. Moreover, one can sometimes be as sure that x as that $\bar{x}$, but one should never be sure that x if and only if $\bar{x}$; and perhaps one might be somewhat sure that x if and only if y, but not as sure that x as that y. But a right to be certain that x if and only if y justifies being as sure that x as that y.)

Is q, then, subjective probability? This question calls for judgment, especially of (d), (e), and, behind them, the counsel of perfection that in making up one's mind about a proposition, one should consider all its consequences. If a subjective view can accommodate these three theses without ceasing to be subjective, then q has a good claim to being subjective probability. But (d) says that R_i, which q represents, is a generalization of logical consequence, and this claim sounds like the leading idea behind logical theories of probability; so if q is subjective probability, what is the difference between logical and subjective probability?

To require that xR_iy when $x \geq y$ is to include logical consequence in i's comparative certainty; but there is enough room left over in R_i for some subjectivity. Here is an example: For a and b in $[0, 1)$ such that $a \leq b$, call

$$[a, b) = \{x \mid a \leq x < b\}$$

the clopen interval from a to b. The set of all subsets of $[0, 1)$ is a Boolean algebra to which all these clopen intervals belong, and the intersection of any two such Boolean algebras is another; so if A is the intersection of all of them, it too is a Boolean algebra to which all these clopen intervals belong. Each member of A is a finite union of pairwise disjoint clopen intervals; $f = [a, a)$, $t = [0, 1)$, and $\geq$, $\vee$, $\wedge$, and $^-$ are the usual set-theoretic relation and functions.

Our example begins with the supposition that a dart is to land in $[0, 1)$. Two people, i and j, are estimating in which member of A the dart might land. Consider, to begin with, only clopen intervals. The first person, i, might think that only the length $b-a$ of $[a, b)$ matters. The second, j, might expect the dart to pull to the right in such a way that its

123

chance of landing in $[a, b)$ is $b^2 - a^2$; j has a quarter confidence in $[0, \frac{1}{2})$, but $\frac{3}{4}$ in $[\frac{1}{2}, 1)$. We will now specify two models, A common to both, which encode i's and j's estimates.

Let q_i be Lebesgue measure on A. Say that $x S_i y$ iff $q_i(x) > q_i(y)$ and that $x T_i y$ iff $q_i(x) = q_i(y)$. Since it is clear that q_i satisfies (a) and (b), the delicate matter is to choose m_i so that

(1) $$q_i(m_i(a, x, y)) = aq_i(x) + (1 - a)q_i(y),$$
(2) $$x \lor y \geq m_i(a, x, y).$$

For any x and y in A, there are unique $b_1, c_1, \ldots, b_n$, $c_n, d_1, e_1, \ldots, d_m, e_m$ in $[0, 1]$ such that

$$x = \bigcup_{p=1}^{n} [b_p, c_p), \qquad b_p \leq c_p < b_{p+1},$$

$$y = \bigcup_{q=1}^{m} [d_q, e_q), \qquad d_q \leq e_q < d_{q+1}.$$

The set of all these clopen intervals, the $[b_p, c_p)$ and the $[d_q, e_q)$ together, splits into two disjoint parts: those clopen intervals any two of which are disjoint, and the rest. For ease of notation, pretend that those of the first sort are the last $n - r$ and $m - s$, respectively. Let

$$U = \bigcup_{p=1}^{n-r} [b_{r+p}, b_{r+p} + a(c_{r+p} - b_{r+p}))$$

$$\cup \bigcup_{q=1}^{m-s} [d_{s+q}, d_{s+q} + (1 - a)(e_{s+q} - d_{s+q})).$$

Then

$$q_i(U) = a \sum_{p=1}^{n-r} (c_{r+p} - b_{r+p}) + (1 - a) \sum_{q=1}^{m-s} (e_{s+q} - d_{s+q})$$

$$= aq_i \left(\bigcup_{p=1}^{n-r} [b_{r+p}, c_{r+p}) \right) + (1 - a)q_i \left(\bigcup_{q=1}^{m-s} [d_{s+q}, e_{s+q}) \right),$$

and because a is in $[0, 1]$,

$$U \subseteq \bigcup_{p=1}^{n-r} [b_{r+p}, c_{r+p}) \cup \bigcup_{q=1}^{m-s} [d_{s+q}, e_{s+q}) \subseteq x \lor y.$$

The set of those of the second sort partitions into u subsets, or clumps $C_1, \ldots, C_u$, such that for each $v = 1, \ldots, u$, each member of C_v is linked to every other member of C_v by overlappings of members of C_v; but if $v \neq w$, $\cup C_v$ and $\cup C_w$ are disjoint. The treatment of C_1 is general enough to illustrate the pattern. Suppose the members of C_1 are $[b_1, c_1), \ldots, [b_k, c_k), [d_1, e_1), \ldots, [d_z, e_z)$. Then let $b = b_1 + \cdots + b_k$, $c = c_1 + \cdots + c_k$, $d = d_1 + \cdots + d_z$, and $e = e_1 + \cdots + e_z$. Let λ_1 be the lesser of b_1 and d_1, and let ρ_1 be $\lambda_1 + a(c - b) + (1 - a)(e - d)$. Then $\lambda_1 \leq \rho_1$, so $[\lambda_1, \rho_1)$ exists. Clearly,

$$q_i([\lambda_1, \rho_1)) = aq_i\left(\bigcup_{p=1}^{k} [b_p, c_p) \right) + (1 - a)q_i\left(\bigcup_{q=1}^{z} [d_q, e_q) \right),$$

and since for this reason the length of $[\lambda_1, \rho_1)$ is between that of $\cup_{p=1}^{k} [b_p, c_p)$ and that of $\cup_{q=1}^{z} [d_q, e_q)$, ρ_1 is less than or equal to the greater of c_k and e_z, so $[\lambda_1, \rho_1) \subseteq \cup C_1$. Therefore, if we set

$$m_i(a, x, y) = U \cup \bigcup_{v=1}^{u} [\lambda_v, \rho_v),$$

then m_i satisfies (1) and (2). [Had we treated clumped intervals as we did disjoint ones, then overlapping might threaten (1); had we treated disjoint intervals as we did clumped ones, the disjointness might threaten (2); so it seems that m_i must be specified from two parts. This construction also shows that the ordinary physical quantity, length, conforms to our general analysis of quantity.]

The function whose value for a nonnegative real argument is its square is finite, increasing, and continuous; let q_j be the Lebesgue–Stieltjes measure on A induced by this function. Say that xS_jy iff $q_j(x) > q_j(y)$ and that xT_jy iff $q_j(x) = q_j(y)$. To specify m_j, proceed as for m_i with two exceptions: to specify U, replace $b_{r+p} + a(c_{r+p} - b_{r+p})$ by $\sqrt{(b_{r+p})^2 + a((c_{r+p})^2 - (b_{r+p})^2)}$, and similarly for $d_{s+q} + (1 - a)(e_{s+q} - d_{s+q})$; to specify ρ_1, let $b = b_1^2 + \cdots + b_k^2$, $c = c_1^2 + \cdots + c_k^2$, $d = d_1^2 + \cdots + d_z^2$, $e = e_1^2 + \cdots + e_z^2$, and let $\rho_1 = \sqrt{\lambda_1^2 + a(c - b) + (1 - a)(e - d)}$.

Each of S_i, T_i, m_i, and S_j, T_j, m_j thus yields a model for all

125

our assumptions, and these two models share the same Boolean algebra, A. Thus, q_i and q_j are i's and j's required estimates. If $x \geq y$, then xR_iy and xR_jy, so $\geq$ is included in both R_i and R_j. But i and j disagree, for $q_i([\frac{1}{2}, 1)) = \frac{1}{2}$, but q_j $([\frac{1}{2}, 1)) = \frac{3}{4}$. According to the logical theory, numerical probability is a unique binary function whose first arguments are bodies of evidence, whose second arguments are elements of a Boolean algebra, and whose range is $[0, 1]$. Its values are the degrees to which evidence entails members of the algebra (propositions), and according to the theory, partial entailment is no less objective than its full-grown variety. Thus, it would seem, according to the logical theory, for each single body of evidence at least one of i and j must be wrong about $[\frac{1}{2}, 1)$. According to the subjective theory, for each rational person there is a unique unary numerical probability function; but there may be as many such functions as there are rational people (even if they all have, or have access to, the same evidence). Tastes, we say, are subjective; there would be nothing untoward were it to happen that i likes chocolate, j dislikes it, and yet neither is in error about any matter of fact or logic. Similarly, a subjective theorist might hold that there is no matter of fact or logic in virtue of which at least one of i and j must be wrong about $[\frac{1}{2}, 1)$, even if they have, or have access to, the same evidence.

The point of this appendix has not been to defend the subjective theory of probability (or the logical theory) but rather to argue that subjective probability, if it exists, requires more than there need be in a person's unique normalized quantity of belief.

9

Psychic energy

Our quantities of belief and desire are founded in a normative conception of rational belief and rational desire. But the norms we required were weak; they impose only the broad structural (in the senses of axioms 1–16) rationality that we have called straightening out. They are compatible with all sorts of motivated irrationalities; for these have more to do, usually at least, with the contents of particular beliefs or particular desires, and with causal relations between particular beliefs and desires, than they have to do with overall linear orderings of beliefs or of desires. As will emerge, such matters are of no little importance if one wishes to come to a just conclusion about whether Freud's economic models have been unfairly, precipitately, or ignorantly consigned to the rubbish bin of intellectual history. The crux of an economic model, in the present state of the art, is whether or not we can make sense of the possibility of psychic energy and, what is necessary for that in the light of our discussion of causation, its conservation at least through wholly intrapsychic processes. (Chemical energy, for example, is not always conserved, since it can be converted to kinetic energy; but chemical energy, to deserve the name, ought to be conserved through wholly chemical processes.)

Wishful thinking is perhaps the most obvious and common-sensical example of motivated irrationality. We find it natural to construe wishful thinking as a person's believing that p because he wants it to be the case that p; in the hackneyed example, the father wishfully thinks that his soldier son missing in action is still alive because he wants his son still to be alive. The view, which has become general in some quarters, that construes this "because" quite literally as adverting to a full-blooded causal nexus between the father's desire and his belief seems correct. Suppose that the father should rationalize (in the pejorative sense) his belief that his son is not dead. That he has rationalized need not be due to any inferior quality in the reasons he states for his belief; even if what he states would be rather good reasons for his belief, he will still be rationalizing if they do not give his real reason for his belief, and that is (only) that he wants his son not to be dead. But following Davidson,[1] it is hard to see how something could be a person's real reason for a belief, and yet not a good reason for it, unless that reason were also a cause of his belief. Hence, it seems natural to suppose that if a person's belief that p is wishful thinking, then he has a desire that p and it bears (at least some of) the causal responsibility for his belief. (This natural supposition is compatible with the father's having acted, perhaps unconsciously or neurotically, in deciding that his son is not dead and with his desire that the son not be dead being both a cause and a reason, indeed a reason because a cause, for his having so acted.)

It is a consequence of the conception of causation defended earlier that quantitative relations should lie at the heart of full-blooded causal relations. Now that we have quantities of desire and belief, we can suggest what sort of quantitative relations might be involved in a causal account of the purest sort of wishful thinking. The obvious suggestion is that when a person's belief that p is wishful thinking of the purest sort, he has a desire that p, and his degree of conviction that p varies directly with (and only with) the strength of his desire that p. (The idea of purity here is explicated by the requirements that only his desire is responsible for his belief. It is a crucial lesson of psychoanalysis that most, if not all, interesting psychological phenomena are overdetermined. So purity is probably an unrealized theoretical idealization of messy reality.)

Following tradition, let us write $u(p)$ for the quantity of the person's desire that p; u is sometimes called utility, and its units are sometimes (horribly) called utiles. Let us write $c(p)$ for the quantity of his belief that p; it might be fun to call c conviction, and its units, convicts. Then an obvious idea for a quantitative law of (pure) wishful thinking might be that there is a constant a such that when his belief that p is (pure) wishful thinking,

$$c(p) = a \cdot u(p).$$

Let us call this the law of pure wishful thinking.

The constant a is one of the intriguing things about this imaginary law. A constant of proportionality between different quantities cannot be a pure number; instead, such a constant may be thought of as a rate at which units of the quantity mentioned on the right are interchangeable with units of the quantity mentioned on the left. In the present case, a would be an amount of convicts per utile.

This utterly elementary consideration is nonetheless suggestive; for though certainly necessary, lawful relations between quantities are not sufficient for causation. The critical nerve of Quine's understanding of causation is flow; and it seems evident that we suppose in wishful thinking a direction of causation from desire to belief. We have as yet represented neither a flow nor its direction in wishful thinking; as far as our imaginary law goes, it could as well describe causation of desire by belief. (Does that ever happen?)

In imagining the law of pure wishful thinking, we supposed a certain uniformity, namely, that there exist a single constant a such that in all of a person's cases of pure wishful thinking that p, $c(p) = a \cdot u(p)$. The obvious way to secure for our fancies about wishful thinking the minima necessary for flow with a direction is to suppose that a is the constant rate (in convicts per utile) at which desire literally converts into belief. The instant that suggestion is made, the only proper question must be: how could that be?

We are, of course, still a long way from being able to ask answerable questions about mechanisms of conversion. The point is rather that our commitment to conservation is such that we are unable to entertain seriously the idea that desire might convert into belief unless we can take seriously the idea that there is some underlying quantity that persists through whatever the processes of conversion might be and that, as it were, begins as a quantity of (the, it is now starting to seem, more superficial) desire but ends as (the perhaps no less superficial) belief; at least that much is built into the very idea of causation as the flow of a conserved quantity along causal chains.[2] If all this is so, the idea of something very much indeed like Freud's notion of psychic energy (though specified from the beginning in purely psychological terms and without any pieties about the glorious future of neurophysiology) seems forced upon us.

In order that your credulity, or at least your willing suspension of disbelief, not be abused, it is important that you understand how very limited are the present claims. We do not claim to have shown that there exists such a quantity as psychic energy. To support such a claim, it would be necessary to specify (in, one would expect, purely psychological, though perhaps now unknown, terms) a quantity conserved through and traceable along (almost) all naïvely identified wholly intrapsychic causal chains. We have specified no such quantity and are, alas, unable to do so; we do not know whether there is such a quantity. Instead, we claim to have exhibited a gap, an absence, a lacuna in our understanding of wishful thinking that would be filled very nicely if there were such a quantity as psychic energy.

We are, perhaps, in a position somewhat analogous to that of physicists in the seventeenth century when Newton was just beginning to think about motion. Descartes had said that the essence of matter is extension. Taking him, as he seems to have intended, literally, this doctrine means that a body is specified by its volume, or perhaps by its shape and its volume. Thus, it would seem that, for Descartes, matter is a geometric phenomenon, and physics is a branch of geometry; putting it that way makes it seem that Descartes was trying to do physics without matter, without solid, impenetrable, ponderable stuff filling out his geometric forms. This oddity marks an important difference between Descartes and Newton. Of all Newton's many great contributions to the wealth of human understanding, the most profound was a quantity. This does not mean his famous articulation of the quantity of velocity at an instant, though that was certainly of decisive importance in making physics possible. It means mass. Newton seems to have been the first man to begin to appreciate the truly profound fact that, for every body, there exists a fixed and constant ratio between the amounts of acceleration produced in it and how hard you have to push it to produce that acceleration. That constant, and not force, is what impresses one most in his second law of motion. This constant (forget Einstein for now) is the body's (inertial) mass, and with mass Newton put back into physics the matter that Descartes had excised. (There are also interesting reasons of principle why, at the beginning of his *Principia,* Newton defines mass as the product of volume and density, but that is another story.)

Thus, in the final quarter of the seventeenth century, Newton was more than reasonably clear about two quantities: velocity at an instant and mass. But we were taught at school that kinetic energy is half the product of mass and the square of velocity. That is a very elementary combination of the basic quantities, and it would be impertinent to suppose that a mathematician of Newton's genius would not have been familiar with that way of combining quantities. But it took approximately two hundred years for the concept of energy to emerge. How can it have taken so long?

The answer, as we have seen before, is conservation. As learned a man as Newton would have been conversant with the idea, handed down through the scholastics from Aristotle and long before, of a conserved quantity traceable along causal chains (though perhaps not expressed in exactly those terms). But it took a long time (and considerable refinements in the precision of the technology available for use in experiments) to amass and understand evidence that there exists such a quantity in Nature, especially when her causal chains cross the boundaries between mechanics and chemistry and electricity and heat and physiology and so on. Only after identifying a conserved quantity traceable along the causal chains within each of these domains, and only after recognizing that each of these quantities converts at a fixed rate to the others through causal chains crossing the boundaries between these areas, only after all that, was someone like Helmholtz justified in signaling out the otherwise boring quantity $\frac{1}{2}mv^2$ for special attention.

Mind in our time is, perhaps, somewhat worse off than matter was in Descartes's. By and large, the prevailing intellectual orthodoxy seems to dismiss the Newton of the mind, namely, Freud. As Descartes denied that the interesting phenomenon, matter, existed, so the prevailing orthodoxy in philosophy denied (or reduced or whatever euphemism) mind in favor of behavior during the two decades after World War II and, during the two subsequent decades, has denied (or whatever) mind in favor of brain.

But in at least one respect our understanding of the mind may not need to be quite so badly obstructed as was Descartes's understanding of matter: whereas Descartes lacked Newton's articulation of mass, the quantity of matter, we have for more than thirty years had von Neumann and Morgenstern's articulation of the quantity of desire. It is probably naïve to hope that it will take less than two hundred years to discern which combination of, perhaps, that quantity and, doubtless, other as yet inarticulate quantities will deserve to be distinguished by some future Helmholtz as psychic energy. Certainly Freud was too wise ever to have published such a claim.

The materialist orthodoxy ought, however, to feel comfortable with a version of psychic energy; for if mental events simply are physical events in the central nervous system, then since that system is a unit within physical nature, energy of presumably a familiar sort courses through that system, causally binding physical events in it and thus the mental events identical with them. There would remain a terminological quibble; for although we would want psychic energy to be specified from the beginning in psychological terms, the orthodoxy might feel ill at ease calling such energies as pass through the central nervous system psychic, and the orthodox would probably expect such energy to be electrochemical.

But it is disingenuous to call this point a quibble, for it conceals an important issue. The most sophisticated version of the materialist orthodoxy is Davidson's token–token identity theory.[3] Let us suppose that there are causal relations between mental and physical events, that where there is causation, there is always natural law, but that there are no strict and deterministic laws on the basis of which mental events (specified as such) can be predicted and explained by physical events (specified as such). Given a particular mental event (specified as such) and a particular physical event that caused the first, there is a law under which the causality between them falls. But since there are no psychophysical laws, this law cannot connect the type of the physical event (the cause) with the mentally specified type of the effect. In order that there be a law connecting cause and effect here, the mental effect must also be of some physical type, and thus a physical event; but no mental type may coincide with a physical type of event. If such a token–token, but not type–type, theory of identity of mental with physical events is true, then though there will be electrochemical energy coursing through the neurons, its flow cannot explain, for example, those causal connections distinctive of wishful thinking; for that would violate the ban on psychophysical laws. Since a principle attraction of Quine's view of causation as energy flow is the naturalistic account of explanation it suggests, and since the flow of electrochemical energy about the central nervous system cannot, according to a token–token identity theory, explain even intrapsychic causal relations, it would be considerably worse than misleading to call such energies psychic. Davidson grants psychophysical (and, presumably, intrapsychic) causation; it is psychophysical law that he denies. So he need not deny that, in wishful thinking, desire causes belief (at least proximately). According to his monism, these desires are identical with certain electrochemical events or states in the central nervous system; call these brain states the *bsd*. The beliefs are also, according to monism, identical with physical states we might call the *bsb* . Anomalousness seems to require that neither the *bsb* nor the *bsd* be natural kinds; for beliefs and desires are psychological kinds, and thus if the *bsb* and the *bsd* were natural kinds, psychophysical laws would seem to follow from the identities required by monism. This in turn more than suggests that there should not be a lawful pattern of flow of electrochemical energy from just the *bsd* to exactly the *bsb*. In this way, anomalousness seems to forbid a scientific explanation of the causal connections distinctive of wishful thinking; materialism will not explain the mind, but instead explain it away.[4]

Of course, the orthodox materialists of whatever sect will deny the dualist thesis that you could be disembodied. Suppose, as a rather wildly speculative aside, that a type–type identity theorist did identify psychic energy with electrochemical energy in the central nervous system. One of the striking features of electricity is the capacity of the electromagnetic field to fill space innocent of gross matter like electrons and quarks and for waves in this field to cross such space. To be sure, we are taught to think sometimes of such emissions as particles called photons; but photons are peculiar particles whose rest mass must be zero, and post-Einstein it might not be lunatic to revise Newton by thinking of *rest* mass as the quantity of matter. What is not obvious is that to identify psychic energy with electrical energy is to be a materialist. But since this sort of speculation tends to get one associated with the lunatic fringe, it is probably not sensible to emphasize it.[5]

We are now in the countdown to liftoff: suppose, just suppose, we could make sense of psychic energy; what could we do with that idea?

10

The senses, part II

Before we digressed from imagining what it would be like to be disembodied, we had furnished the disembodied person with veridical visual experience. But that was not sufficient for him to be able to see. Sight requires veridical visual experience caused by that in virtue of which it is veridical, and perhaps via the medium of light. Causation, we argued, is the flow of energy; the flow of energy requires its conservation, which is a quantitative principle; and there are intrinsically psychological quantities of, for example, belief and desire. Can we now start putting the pieces together so as to imagine a disembodied person having veridical visual experience caused by that in virtue of which it is veridical and through the medium of light?

We located (at least part of) the disembodied person at the region of convergence of his lines of sight, that is, those lines along which things seem to him to spread out from him, so seeming because of his visual experience, and along which they actually do spread out, actually, because his experience is veridical. So suppose that when light arrives from those objects along those lines at that region of convergence, it passes straight on through, but it loses some of its energy. At the same time, certain quantities in the disembodied person increase. It would be best to be able to ask you to suppose that, first, he comes to have enough psychic energy that his visual experience continues because of his having that psychic energy; second, his visual experience causes him to have or to sustain some of his beliefs about the objects of which those experiences are veridical; third, the psychic energy implicated

136

in the degree of conviction with which he holds or sustains those beliefs comes from the psychic energy implicated in the veridical visual experience that caused or sustained those beliefs; and fourth, the psychic energy implicated in his veridical visual experience comes from the energy lost by the light (where his visual experience is veridical because it so derives its energy). But most of the quantitative parts of this supposition are promissory notes we cannot redeem. So, at least officially, you are asked to suppose that when light arriving at the region of convergence loses energy, his visual experience continues, and continues to sustain some of his beliefs about those objects of which his experience is veridical, and that there is a fixed rate of conversion between the quantity of energy lost by the light and the degree of those convictions he continues to have about those objects. (It is not that there are not quantities in, say, the intensity of experience; doubtless, there are. But we have not yet articulated them even as well as we have articulated the quantity of conviction.)[1]

The core of this supposition is the fixed rate of conversion between the amount of energy lost by the light and the degree of conviction got by the disembodied person;[2] for how could that be unless fundamental energy, itself potentially either physical or mental, that had been in the light did not vanish into nothing, which would violate the conservation of energy, but has been transformed and continues as a degree of conviction (and its psychic energy)? If so, we have all but conceived of a flow of energy from objects in virtue of which visual experience is veridical, initially a flow via the transmission of light and ending a bit past the veridical visual experience of those objects. We may conclude that the causal conditions necessary for sight in disembodied people can, probably, be met.

This construction needs examination, but before examining it, we should sketch briefly its analogues for the other four senses. Consider the region an inch or two below the region of convergence of the disembodied person's lines of sight and about an inch across. Suppose that when complex, aromatic molecules drift into this region (from, say, some nearby, freshly ground coffee), they drift straight through but they lose some of the electrochemical energies binding them together, so that it is actually their simpler fragments that drift straight out the other side. At the same time, the disembodied person undergoes olfactory experiences just like those you have when you smell freshly ground coffee. He comes for that reason to believe that there is freshly ground coffee nearby, and there is a fixed ratio between the amount of the conviction that he thus acquires and the electrochemical binding energy lost by the aromatic molecules breaking up. That could be what true belief from veridical olfactory experience caused by that in virtue of which it is veridical might be like in the disembodied, so they could smell. Consider next a region about an inch below this, about as wide and two inches or so deep. When molecules of salt, sugar, lemon juice, aloe juice, and many other stuffs drift into this region, they lose electrochemical binding energy and break up, and the simpler fragments drift straight out the other side. At the same time, at least if enough molecules pass through and break up, the disembodied person has gustatory experiences, that is, salty, sweet, sour, or bitter tastes, or so on as the case may be. These cause him to form (typically) true beliefs that there is salt, sugar, lemon juice, aloe juice, or so on as the case may be in the offing, and there is a fixed ratio between the amount of electrochemical binding energy lost by the molecules breaking up and the amount of the (true) conviction he acquires. That could be what true belief from veridical gustatory experience caused by that in virtue of which it is veridical might be like in the disembodied, so they could taste.

These regions front in a common plane. Perpendicular to that plane are two planes, one on each side of these regions and about four inches or so apart. In each of the two planes, a few inches behind the first plane and in altitude (most often) between that of the region where lines of sight converge and light loses energy, on the one hand, and, on the other, the region whose aromatic molecules break up, there is a region with the following properties. When sound waves arrive there from, say, a ringing bell two hundred feet to the right, they lose vibratory (that is, kinetic) energy but pass straight through; at the same time, the disembodied person has an auditory experience just like the one you would have if you heard that ringing of that bell from the area of the places described. This experience causes him to believe that there is a bell ringing, and when sound loses energy at both places, his auditory experiences cause him to believe that the bell is about two hundred feet to the right. There is a fixed ratio between the kinetic energy lost by the sound waves passing through these regions and the amounts of the true convictions he has thus acquired. That could be what true belief from veridical auditory experience caused by that in virtue of which it is veridical might be like in the disembodied, so they could hear.

In each of these cases we should also have told a story like that in Chapter 3 about you, still (mostly) embodied but seeing in the mirror that, first, your eyes have gone, then your brain, and finally the rest of your body. For instance, imagining away your ears, you could imagine hearing your finger probe the empty channels in your head where once your tympanum, anvil, stirrup, and so on were. You can make up three such gruesome stories for yourself, one each for your ears, nose, and mouth and tongue. But some seem to find touch a bit more difficult to treat similarly.

The recipe for making up such stories is to speculate about how conservation of energy might apply to the embodied sense with its usual organ and then to transpose those speculations into the disembodied mode. In the case of embodied touch, the usual organ is (at least) the skin, which is spread over the whole surface of the body. When lumps of matter smack into or rub along the skin, they bounce off (if we are lucky), losing, one supposes, some kinetic energy in the process. That energy turns up in amounts of true conviction about the shape, texture, hardness, temperature, speed, and so on of the matter with which the body collided.

To transpose this speculation into the disembodied mode requires us to solve two problems. First, we must not cheat; that is, we must not turn the disembodied into invisible men. H. G. Wells's invisible man, as played by Claude Rains in the film, still had a material body that shaped his clothes; it was just an invisible body. We must not suppose moving objects to bounce off the disembodied, for that would be to attribute impenetrability by matter to them, and impenetrability by matter is a hallmark of matter. But it would not be cheating to suppose that whenever objects, however light and however slow, pass through the region occupied by the disembodied person, they lose some fraction of their speed but pass straight through without his acquiring any motion; for that puts his "mass" below all positive lower bounds, and thus he still lacks a material body.

No two objects of the same kind can occupy exactly the same place at the same time, so since any two material objects are, in the relevant sense, of the same kind, no two material objects can fill the same place at once. But according to the present account, an enormous boulder may come to fill the volume of space occupied by a disembodied person; if he is to feel it, the boulder may do so a bit more slowly than you might have expected, but it may nonetheless do so. Hence, the disembodied person is not of the same kind as any material object; thus, he lacks a material body. (It should, by the way, be obvious from geometric objects, like the sphere of radius one mile centered at the midpoint of the segment joining the centers of mass of the earth and the moon, that merely having location in space and volume is not sufficient for being material.) The story of disembodied touch then continues. At the same time as matter passing through him loses kinetic energy, he has veridical tactual experiences that cause in him true beliefs whose quantity of conviction bears a fixed ratio to the kinetic energy lost by the objects in virtue of which his beliefs are true. But at least one problem remains: how do we imagine away the organ of touch, and what is the relevant region?

Most philosophy students have heard stories about the phantom limbs of amputees. Imagine first that when you awake, your arm (only) is missing, but it feels (in your phantom arm) just as if your arm were there and against the bedclothes. Your phantom arm drifts through the mattress; but then it feels to you there (in your phantom arm) just as if your arm were there among the bits of stuffing in the mattress. Indeed, when your phantom hand drifts (drifts because we have not got as far as action yet) to the surface of your phantom shoulder, there is in each a feeling as if each were there touching the other. Now generalize; instead of a phantom arm, imagine you have a phantom body. The region at least over the surface of which you are sensitive is the relevant region. So the sense of touch could survive in a disembodied person.

By the sensations, we mean feelings like itches, pain, tickles, perhaps hunger, and (the feelings of) orgasm. They are distinguished from perceptual experiences, and perhaps from all other mental states, by not being intensional, that is, by not being *of* something else. To be sure, they have their parts in the evolutionary economy of the body: pain can warn us of bodily injury; hunger prompts us to fuel the fleshy engine; and orgasm, rewarding animals who tend toward reproduction, will thus tend to be inherited. But in the way that a holiday memory is transparently a memory *of* Wales, a mental image, an image *of* Shangrila (which, note, does not exist), or a tactual experience, an experience *of* a rough, warm surface, in that way a headache is not *of,* does not present us with, sludge in the vessels of the head, nor does hunger present us with an empty belly, nor is an itch *of* some who knows not what. The sensations seem to be capable of tying into

141

action in some more primitive way than perceptual experience. Perception typically issues in belief, which, with desire, informs decision, which issues in action. But pain, especially, can simply bypass deliberation and yet issue in actions as opposed to reflex movements like peristalsis. Whatever this more primitive but not quite reflex tie with action might be, it seems to relieve the sensations of any need to represent, whereas perceptual experience, as the input to deliberation, needs to represent if deliberation is to be useful by representing correctly.[3]

Nonetheless, we do seem to tend to think of sensation with perceptual experience, and with tactual experience in particular. It seems plain that once you have swallowed your phantom body, or rather the idea of it, you should have no additional difficulty imagining having a headache in your phantom head or an itch in your phantom left ear. (Of course, the possibility is in a way horrid, for how could you scratch?) Note that if the sensations indeed do not represent, then veridicality has no purchase on them, and thus there is no problem about how they might be caused in disembodied people by that in virtue of which they are veridical. Because sensations are (in a perplexing way) more primitive than perceptual experience, it is easier to imagine what sensations would be like even though you have no body than it is to imagine perception. We may conclude that disembodied people could experience any sensations of which we are capable.

The phantom body also gives us a way to answer a stimulating question: do the disembodied have gender? It is probably inadequate to cite desire and the appetites, thinking that disembodied people who desired embodied men would be women, and vice versa; it is enough to remember homosexuality to see why. It might be more commonsensical to say that as gender in the embodied is fixed by genitals molded out of flesh, so phantom genitals fix gender in the disembodied. But, of course, an objector could respond by asking about the possibility of what is called transsexuality, a person of one sex in a body anatomically of the other sex; if that really happens, and if it is as simple as that description suggests, it is hard to see how to understand it except in terms, perhaps, of appetites and delusions, and that seems to take us back to our first answer. But these matters are murky enough even among the embodied that perhaps we need not be embarrassed to have no final answer.

One difference between our dualism and Descartes's should now be emerging. Because he concentrated so on the higher or intellectual faculty of thinking, and because he seems merely to have succumbed to embarrassment when asked about give and take between mind and matter, it is all too easy to get an almost otherworldly idea of a Cartesian *res cogitans* as utterly cut off from the cavortings of geometric nature; despite his famous appeal to the pineal gland, it is not absolutely clear that the master even took quite seriously the problem of locating the *res cogitans* in space. However, even having considered only perception and sensation, faculties he did not make much of and may have thought bodily, it is patent that a disembodied person could not possibly interact causally with what he, say, sees unless there are changes in the light by means of which he sees when that light reaches the region of convergence of his lines of sight and loses some of its energy there; for this is a change in the light, and some such change must occur if the energy flow view of causation is correct. It follows that where there is a disembodied person in whom all five senses are working, there will be changes in matter or familiar sorts of energy. It would be a cheat to suppose these changes too small to be detected by us embodied sorts. So you might be able to see where a disembodied person, or part of him, is by, let us imagine, a sort of dimming of the light there; you might be able to feel where he is because, although you can pass through his location, your transit is slowed just that noticeable little bit. The upshot is that in order that disembodied people should be able to perceive, we should conceive of them more like the ghost of traditional folklore, more like Casper the Friendly

143

Ghost, than like Cartesian unworldly intellects. So long as we can fend off the merchants of ectoplasm (an intellectual confusion because only material objects are parcels of stuff, however subtle), this link between dualism properly understood and the simplicities of folklore seems a sort of common sense.

This result has consequences for dualism and the metaphysics of personal identity. We mentioned the latter problem briefly and in passing when in Chapter 3 we treated what we called the *de dicto* objection. To begin in this general area, suppose someone asks whether a dualist holds sensible views about the problem of personal identity. The objection implicit in this question has been put as follows: "The most that follows from what I can imagine is that someone psychologically like me, someone in a situation 'epistemically indistinguishable' from mine, could become disembodied. This is a claim of *de dicto* possibility. And there is no way to get from this to the *de re* possibility claim that I am such that it is possible for me to exist disembodied."[4] Some changes in oneself are unproblematic to imagine; it is easy to imagine being a bit richer or a bit taller than one is in fact, and this convinces us that we could be a bit richer or a bit taller than we in fact are. Other changes are more difficult to imagine. Can one imagine so changing as to have the body, the sensations, and the thoughts, if any, of an alligator or a sponge? Could any alligator or sponge one imagines be oneself? Some are dubious. Similarly, the objector urges, though perhaps one can imagine a disembodied person mentally just like oneself, one cannot imagine one's genuine self, as it were, to be disembodied. How does the dualist know that it is he himself who persists through the disembodiment he imagines?

Some people lack eyes, and each of us could lose his eyes; we are convinced of this because each of us can imagine what it would feel like not to have eyeballs in his eye sockets. Here, no worry about whether it is our genuine selves we are imagining seems sensible. In this story, as in imagining being a bit richer, it seems in no way problematic simply to suppose that

144

it is ourselves to whom the change occurs. Now recall how we began to imagine becoming disembodied, that is, how we might see although disembodied. We imagined that, still embodied, we cross to the mirror one morning before raising our eyelids, and then, having raised our lids, we see in the mirror that our eye sockets are empty. You can visualize how your face would then look in the mirror. You can imagine having visual experience without eyes; and there is no evident ground for worrying about whether it is really you whom you are imagining to have this experience. It is evident that this is as much a possibility genuinely about oneself as any other; if you like, stare at yourself in the mirror to fix yourself in mind before you close your eyes to begin imagining. (It is simply a confusion to identify the distinction between *de dicto* and *de re* possibility with the distinction between epistemic and genuine possibility; epistemic possibility has never been in question with us.)

We then extended the story in two different ways. First, we built up from visual experience to vision, most importantly by adding veridicality and causation by that in virtue of which the visual experience is veridical. Along this way, there is no evident ground on which we lose our grip on its being our genuine selves to whom this is imagined to happen. Second, after imagining seeing that we have lost our eyes, we then imagined opening our skulls and seeing that our brains are also gone; and it seems hardly problematic that we imagine of our genuine selves that we persist through the loss of a bodily organ, even the brain. Then, having imagined away our eyes and our brains, the two bodily organs usually thought most intimately connected with vision, we proceeded down the second way by imagining away, bit by bit if you like, all the rest of the body. It may be this last that prompts worry about personal identity, about whether it is still our genuine selves we are at the end imagining.

It may not be plain to one who is innocent of theory why worries about personal identity might arise just here, so we need some theory. People have ages as well as volumes. The problem of personal identity is sometimes exposited by directing attention to the instantaneous stages of a person's history and asking in virtue of what relation two such are stages in the history of a single person. One account of this relation concentrates on later stages, including memories, perhaps of a special sort, of experiences in earlier stages. Another sort of account concentrates on spatiotemporal continuity from the earlier to the later stages.

Were either relation between stages necessary for personal identity, the dualist could easily help himself to it. This is patent for the memory sort of account. But it is also true of continuity accounts; for although continuity is typically described in terms of *bodily* continuity through space and time, it need not be. We took trouble to locate our disembodied selves in space; so all that need be required for a continuity account is a spatiotemporally continuous person through disembodiment, and that was already part of our story, even if we saw no reason to emphasize it. Furthermore, because on our account disembodied people resemble ghosts whose locations another person could detect, that person could also trace us spatiotemporally continuously through disembodiment. To begin with, we were where our bodies were; while we remain, we imagine our bodies away bit by bit; finally we have imagined our genuine selves to have remained there continuously after all the body is gone.

But even this much concedes too much to the objection. Any orderly exposition of concepts must begin somewhere, and the concept of identity seems about as basic as concepts get. So why not say that stages are stages of the same person precisely in case they are stages of the same person? There is for the dualist no problem that requires the reduction of identity for persons to some other relation between momentary stages of persons. Memory and continuity may have an epistemic role; they may be a relevant sort of *evidence* that a person encountered at one time is the same person as a person

146

encountered at another. But since we can forget, memory hardly seems to be what being the same person consists in; and since we can imagine being intermittent, neither is spatiotemporal continuity. If one likes, one might say that identity is the smallest reflexive relation; but since even that seems hardly explanatory, it seems better to take identity, and thus identity of persons, as primitive. (The remarks in this paragraph stem from a talk by a distinguished philosopher who has not published it, so it seems inadvisable to saddle him with our exposition by crediting his ideas to him by name.) The upshot is that personal identity is no more problematic for the dualist than for anyone else.

Of course, there is not a jot of good evidence that there actually are ghosts; the commonsense appeal of disembodiment on the model of ghosts in folklore is purely conceptual, and indeed once dualism is properly understood, it is not clear that it would be at all pleasant to be disembodied. But that is beside the point. Dualism is a *modal* thesis about the possibility of being disembodied; that it should never actually happen would be no objection to dualism whatsoever. (And there are schools of thought that would attach importance to the fact that the actuality of disembodiment has been shown to be falsifiable. Quite apart from whether there are ghosts, there is a genuine experimental question about whether the total amount of electrochemical energy in the central nervous system remains constant over suitably selected intervals of time or manifests otherwise inexplicable variations, perhaps especially in the neighborhood of the pineal gland, that are incompatible with the conservation of familiar sorts of energy.)

Some have objected by distinguishing information and energy and claiming that a sense works by receiving information about the environment rather than by absorbing sheer quantities of energy from it. It is difficult to respond to an objection that is both correct and nonexistent. That is, it is true that to see is not simply to absorb energy from light in

147

the way that a rock lying in the sun gets hot. But this does not mean that to acquire information about what you see is something utterly divorced from absorbing energy from light reflected from what you see to you. We do not yet understand much about what information in the relevant sense is. But perhaps it is not an irresponsible speculation to suggest that an informative signal is a packet of energy patterned in certain ways (which we can now articulate only roughly and in a few cases), that the patterning is a matter not so much of amount per se of energy, but of differences between the amounts like frequencies or wavelengths in different parts (spatial or temporal) of the packet, and that to learn or acquire information when the packet arrives is for enough of it to be converted to your sort of energy and in such a way that these differentials are preserved. When the rock in the sun gets hot, distinctions between the wavelengths of the light arriving are lost when the energy goes over into more or less uniform jiggling of molecules in the crystal of the rock. But when light strikes your retina, these distinctions are not lost because your rods and cones respond differently to different wavelengths; you see color and acquire information. That is not because you do not absorb energy, but because you do, only in a pattern-preserving (or reconstructing) way. If we understood it in our embodied case, we might for all we know be able to transpose it into the disembodied mode; but it hardly seems fair to require us to do what no one can do in the familiar case. What is the relation between the pattern of pressures on your skin and the wealth of differences between different parts of the *feel* of your loved one's skin to you? Until that question is answered there is no objection to answer; and when answered, we may for all we know be able to transpose it into the disembodied mode.

Then, too, there will be those who object that anything that interacts causally with matter is for that very reason alone matter. There is, of course, no answering such an objection, for it is merely a transformation of the claim that there can be no causal interaction between mind and matter unless the mind is matter. It is as if you were asked to prove that there are infinitely many primes, and when you had rehearsed Euclid's argument, someone objected by asserting flatly that there are only finitely many primes. Perhaps the most tactful response would be to say that the objection begs the question and leave it at that.

But what probably underlies the objection is a question: how can electromagnetic energy in light be converted to a quantity of conviction? That is a real question that deserves all honor, and that we cannot answer. But then neither can the orthodox materialist. Should we be any more embarrassed by our ignorance than he is by his? (Neurophysiology, however glorious its future may be, will never answer this question unless it tells us something, sometime, about belief.) We all know that when an atom bomb explodes, some matter is converted to energy. But how? As far as one can see, we do not know. We do seem to know the rate at which one exchanges for the other, and that seems to make us feel justified in talking about mass–energy. Analogously, we imagine that electromagnetic energy in light converts at a fixed rate to conviction in the disembodied. That should make us feel justified in thinking that there could be a more fundamental sort of energy, now perhaps physical but with the capacity to become mental. Since we have other reasons for thinking that the disembodied person is nonetheless not physical (for the densest boulder or neutron star can fill his volume without disloging him), there is no reason to be more embarrassed by our ignorance than the orthodox materialist is by his.

It seems plausible to suppose that as, over the past two millennia or so, a belief in ghosts has proved increasingly insupportable, the idea of the soul as the vehicle of immortality has been increasingly rarified by wishful thinking. Although it will usually be too tactful to express the contempt merited, good sense has by now neither patience with nor respect for a faith in the actual existence of either ghosts or the immortal soul when such faith is rooted in wishful thinking (as opposed to filial piety). As for the wish behind the thinking, the ancient poets who said that the most fortunate people are those who were never born at all probably got it about right. As for the metaphysics, the possibility of ghosts that never actually part from their material counterparts still has something to teach us about the nature of the mind.[5]

11

Propositional attitudes

But there is still a gaping hole in the fabric of our imaginings. It is the empty place that ought to be occupied by belief. Let us review our thinking about location.

We began by placing (part of) the disembodied person at the region of convergence of his lines of sight in his veridical visual experience. Later we supplemented his location by appeal to his other veridical sensory experience and, more importantly, by the places where fractions of familiar energy vanish (by being converted to his psychic energy). This last is most important because it reduces our need to locate him by appeal to the content of his experience. Such a reduction is desirable because locating him by the content of his experience may require some reasoning in need of strict scrutiny.

We never attributed a location to his experience, only to him or parts of him. But the reasoning at issue here will emerge more clearly if we pretend that we attributed a location to his veridical visual experience. The suspect mode of inference is exemplified by calling a veridical visual experience of a red thing a red experience. It is in general fallacious to reason that because an experience (whether veridical or not) is of something's having a certain property, that experience itself has the property in question. Something can look to be made out of wood or feel to be heavier than your father; but no visual experience is made out of wood (even if materialism be true), nor is any tactual experience heavier than your father.

Hence, not all predicates figuring in the specification of the content of experience, even veridical experience, are true of that experience; to make the point more graphic, calling an experience of something red a red experience might be thought of as pulling out a predicate; then the point is that not all predicates can be pulled out. But it does not follow from this point that no predicates can ever be pulled out.

It is very difficult to resist the analogy between photographs and visual experiences, and since a photograph of a wooden object heavier than your father is doubtless neither itself wooden nor heavier than your father, photographs are like visual experiences in that not all the predicates figuring in the specification of their content can be pulled out. But a photograph of a man about six feet away facing front at least once was about six feet before him facing toward him. So, it would seem, in the case of photographs, something like the converses of some relational spatial predicates can be pulled out and applied to the photograph. Hence, it may not be a crime against the general prohibition on pulling out predicates to locate veridical visual experience by its content, by the point of view from which things appear to one having that experience.

Causation is the flow of energy. The flow of a quantity is its specifically local, rather than global, conservation; and no quantity can be locally conserved unless it is located in space. Sight, we said, is veridical visual experience caused by that in virtue of which it is veridical, so to imagine a disembodied person seeing, we had to imagine energy (coming in with light) flowing to where his veridical visual experience is located. Consequently, we need to suppose that his veridical visual experience is located in space; and we must also suppose that the "psychic energy" got by his veridical visual experience (to balance the books for the energy lost by the light) is also located in space. The phrase "psychic energy" is still a promissory note that may not be redeemed for centuries, so although it is obvious that there must be quantities of some sort specific to visual experience, this part of the story must, for now, remain sheer fantasy. But like Melville's interleaved chapters on the natural history of leviathan, we did try to sustain your willing suspension of disbelief by offering genuine coin of the realm, the quantity of conviction. When in the story the light lost energy, it was a gesture toward balancing the books for the sake of causation that the quantity of conviction increased. But this will not be authentic causation, the *flow* of energy, unless the quantity of conviction is *locally* conserved. The local conservation of conviction seems clearly to require that a person's beliefs be located in space. Of course, that the disembodied should be able to see requires only that their veridical visual experience be caused by that in virtue of which it is veridical, not that their true beliefs, formed on the basis of veridical experience, be caused by that in virtue of which they are true. But even if strictly speaking the story does not need it, the story seems to limp if we can only locate experience from which we cannot articulate an authentic quantity and we cannot locate belief from which we can articulate such a quantity. Being legalistic usually masks crime.

The problem is that although we can locate experience, it is not clear that there is any such thing as experience of one's own beliefs or any of one's own propositional attitudes. Is there such a thing as introspection, what Kant called inner sense, which can be turned upon our propositional attitudes and in whose exercise we have experience that we can locate by way of approximating to locating the propositional attitudes it reveals to us?

We do, of course, form beliefs about our own beliefs; such second-order beliefs are necessary (but not sufficient) for the first-order belief, as it were, to be conscious. We could suppose a quantitative law of consciousness, that is, that there are constants a_1 and a_2 such that when the belief that p or the desire that q is conscious, there is a belief r_p in the first case that one believes that p, or r_q in the second case that one desires that q, and $c(r_p) = a_1 \cdot c(p)$ or $c(r_q) = a_2 \cdot u(q)$. Were such a law true, it might be evidence that there is a faculty of

153

introspection and that it works causally. But it would not be good evidence that introspection is an inner *sense;* for we have as yet no reason to believe that there is any such thing as experience of one's belief that p or desire that q. Without such experience we seem no closer to locating the propositional attitudes.

To digress for a moment, one supposes that there might also be a quantitative law of unconsciousness, that is, that there are constants a_1' and a_2' such that when the belief that p or the desire that q is unconscious, then, first, $c(p)$ or $u(q)$ will typically be rather large, this probably figuring in the motives for wanting to keep them out of consciousness. Second, there will be a belief r_p in the first case that one believes that p, or r_q in the second case that one desires that q, these, as Sartre noted, doubtless being necessary in order that repression be a genuine action, as it must be, and thus requiring one to believe oneself to have that which one wants to repress. But third, though $c(r_p) = a_1' \cdot c(p)$ or $c(r_q) = a_2' \cdot u(q)$ as before, and though a_1' and a_2' must not be of such a size as to threaten the existence of r_p or r_q', one expects a_1' to be rather smaller than a_1, and a_2', than a_2, in order that the belief that p or the desire that q be unconscious. Presumably the psychic energy that would in a case of consciousness have gone to animate r_p or r_q has in cases of unconsciousness been bled off into the action of repression;[1] a good account of repression would balance the books. Now let us return from psychoanalysis to philosophy.

It is not that there is any special problem about whether disembodied people could engage in the higher mental functions. Indeed, belief and desire, thought and emotion, imagining and remembering, rage, fear, envy, pride, and greed, and hope and love, dreaming and planning, and contemplation, musing and reasoning, and so on through the hard-to-survey canon of the higher faculties, the propositional attitudes, none of these seems to us who engage in them to make enough use of the body for there to be any obstacle whatsoever to our imagining ourselves engaging in them when disembodied. Descartes knew what he was doing when he said that he was a being whose essence it is to *think*.

But that thesis has odd consequences for sleep.² What would be the difference between the dreamless sleep of the disembodied and their temporary nonexistence? The question is unsettling only so long as one identifies the mind with the conscious mind, an identification sometimes motivated by an idealism with respect to the mind, that is, by the view that our mental states are dependent for their existence on our consciousness of them. Such idealism with respect to the mind is at best uncongenial beside the fact of the unconscious. But to appeal to the contents of the unconscious to distinguish the dreamless sleep of the disembodied (or, for that matter, those no less embodied than you) from their temporary nonexistence is still to concede too much to idealism: it is to concede that a mind without contents cannot exist, and that is Hume's bundle theory of the self; but since there is no understanding how a mere container of mental states could be an agent, as you are the agent when you imagine or decide, the bundle theory should be resisted, as most reductionist theories in philosophy should be resisted, even though we are all like Hume in having no introspective experience of our selves. (The idea of the transcendence of the ego is an epistemic truth.) When a person is dreamlessly asleep, his mind is inactive; but no substance, not even the mind, is reducible to the actual exercise of its powers. But in what, it may be asked, does the existence of a disembodied person dreamlessly asleep *consist?* The phrase "consist in" should always make one suspect reductionism, so here it seems fair to answer: actual psychic energy, which is potential, perhaps, in the way that a still, heavy object high up is said to have lots of potential energy but none the less actual for that.

Now let us return to our problem: whether we have experiences of our own propositional attitudes. It seems that for at least most of our propositional attitudes most of the time, there is no such thing as an experience of them; by and large, inner sense of propositional attitudes does not exist. (We say no more than "most" and "by and large" because we are not quite certain of the relation between the propositional attitude of imagining that Caesar crossed the Rubicon in 49 B.C. and a mental image of Caesar crossing the Rubicon in 49 B.C.; it is not quite clear whether the latter is an experience or something of which we can have an experience.)

The claim is experimental; that is, when you are clear about what it means, you will realize that it is borne out by your own mental life. Take what should be an example favorable to an opponent whom we shall suppose; take the thought that the planet Jupiter is larger than the planet Mars. The opponent forms (his version of) this thought; we ask him to examine his thought. But, we say to him, he should be careful not to form images of the planets Jupiter and Mars; or if he does, then he must be careful to leave out their shapes, colors, and everything else, except their sizes. After all, the thought is a thought about only their sizes, not their shapes, colors, and so forth. To try to articulate the point, experiencing one's mental images cannot be experiencing one's thoughts. That could be so only if for each image there were exactly one sentence (up to synonymy) that put it into words, and for each sentence there were exactly one image that it puts into words; for propositional attitudes are specified in the first instance by that-clauses that are sentences. But both correspondences fail. Given an image, there is no (clear-cut) end to the words into which it might, more or less, be put; and two stories into which it might be (more or less) put can differ and yet there be no fact of the matter which of the two better renders the image. Since images usually do not have isolable verbs, it is at least not unambiguous what an image means to assert, ask, command, suppose, or what not. Conversely, most sentences truly describing an object do not settle points that an image of it must settle one way or another. The opponent's thought was a thought only about the

156

sizes of Jupiter and Mars, not about their shapes. But what could an image of them in their respective sizes but omitting anything to do with shape be like? So since the content of a propositional attitude is specified by a sentence in a that-clause (at least, typically or most explicitly), we cannot count on being able to trade the sentence in for a mental image the having of which or the experiencing of which will be experiencing the propositional attitude.

But if there are not tight enough correspondences between sentences and images of their subject matter (leaving out the question of sentences whose subject matter is too abstract, like the natural models of ZF, for any image), then, says the opponent, why not just visualize an inscription of the sentence that gives the content of the attitude? But one can visualize inscriptions of Hebrew, Chinese, or Russian sentences that one does not understand; so visualizing inscriptions of sentences does not suffice for having any propositional attitude. (This holds even if someone tells one what a single Russian sentence means in English; for even if Pavlov conditions one to feel hungry on hearing a bell and thereafter one associates the two, it is false that hearing a bell is, in one, feeling hungry.) One might in visualizing an inscription of the sentence "Jupiter is larger than Mars" attend only to its calligraphy and, indeed, ignoring what it is about, have no astronomical thoughts (or other propositional attitudes) at all. Conversely, it seems quite usual to be pleased that your friends have just arrived without being distracted by mental images of sentences. (Do not let some theory force you into saying that there must be an unconscious image of a sentence unless you have some reason other than the theory for supposing there to be such an image; and if the image is unconscious, what becomes of the experience of the propositional attitude?)

Once one realizes that neither a mental image of the subject matter of the sentence specifying the content of a propositional attitude nor an image of an inscription of that sentence

157

is experience of that propositional attitude, then because no plausible (or even implausible) third alternative occurs, it is natural to conclude that for most of the propositional attitudes, that is, for most of the higher mental functions, there is no such thing as an experience of them. It was the later Wittgenstein who most emphasized this fact of experience (or, perhaps better, its absence). Over and over in the later corpus, he asks the interlocutor to attend carefully to his mental state, being also careful to ignore irrelevant images and sensations. For years, the prejudice (also, alas, abetted by Wittgenstein) that philosophy cannot be empirical and the prejudice that introspection is not respectable, prejudices that so much go without saying as to escape critical scrutiny, can lead one either to ignore the injunction to attend to one's experience or to fail to consider seriously the significance of the results of the experiments. But, now, when one does perform the experiment, one discovers in oneself no such thing as an experience of a propositional attitude.

But what does this mean? That there are no propositional attitudes, no beliefs, thoughts, hopes, and fears? No; but it has the consequence that if we know that we have beliefs, thoughts, hopes, and fears, we do not know this by experiencing our beliefs, thoughts, hopes, and fears; for there is no such experience. But we are all of us empiricists in our bones (even, or especially, Plato); we do not understand knowledge otherwise than as acquired through experience of its subject matter. This does not mean that we believe that there is no knowledge except that acquired or justified by experience of its subject matter; an unprejudiced reading of the history of science convinces us otherwise. But an unprejudiced reading of the history of the philosophy of science (which goes back to Plato, and probably, before) should convince us that this is the only sort of knowledge we comfortably think we understand. So we are confronted by the specter of skepticism about self-knowledge; is it even possible to obey the ancient injunction to know thyself? How?

158

What does one really experience in oneself during conversation? While your friend speaks aloud to you, words, phrases, or sentences may go through your mind. You may repeat silently to yourself bits and snatches of what he says, perhaps because they are striking or so that when they vanish, it will be into whatever memory is that they vanish. You may start to say things silently to yourself in preparation for your turn to speak aloud to him; but good manners, good sense, and good tactics require that your silent speech interrupt his overt discourse as little as possible. Mostly, all you do is listen to what he says; and then his overt, public utterances are at the focus of your attention. This experience is nothing but hearing, and in this hearing what you attend to are the words you hear. There are not two things, his words and your hearing of them, that you experience; all you attend to are his words. When your turn comes to speak, then, especially at the start or at difficult points, you may pause and try out a word, phrase, or sentence in silent speech into your mind's ear. But when you are in full spate, mostly you do not; mostly all you attend to in yourself is your own speech. Where do the words come from? They seem just to come.

What certainly is not true is that one first experiences with the mind's eye or ear or nose or whatnot some pre- or nonverbal thought, that one second devises in silent speech English sentences that one compares with the nonverbal or pre-English thought to determine which sentence expresses the thought least inaccurately, and that one third utters the least bad aloud. One does not experience two mental things, one a nonverbal or pre-English thought, and the other a sentence in silent speech. At most, one may experience in oneself silent speech that, sometimes, one edits in talking aloud; and usually, all there is in one for one to attend to is what one says aloud. This does not mean that there are no nonverbal or pre-English thoughts; it means that in conversation, one experiences no such thoughts.

Of course, we sometimes struggle to express ourselves, to

find words to say what we mean. But what exactly is the experience of that like? The struggle itself is an experience of absence, which is, it seems, precisely an absence of experience (except for discomfort, which is irrelevant). Nothing comes to the mind's ear; then, sometimes, something does come. A word, phrase, or sentence occurs to us. There might as well be a feeling of relief, but it cannot always be trusted. It seems that the best evidence for whether what occurred to us does or does not express us, does or does not say what we mean, lies not in measuring it against some nonverbal or pre-English thought, but in how the conversation goes on after we have uttered aloud what came to us. Are earlier obscurities now clarified? Are previously apparently disconnected points now clearly and interestingly related to one another? Do good new things now start to occur to you and your partner in conversation? (Conscious and articulate thinking, especially about complex or difficult matters, is often quite like conversation except that you are identical with your partner.)

The experience of having a word on the tip of your tongue but being unable to think of it is an absence of experience. The folk wisdom, which seems the best strategy, for this distressing state is: don't worry about it; do something else; don't try to remember. Then, when you least expect it, it often just pops into your head. Sometimes, if you can resist forcing it, you can free-associate to it. You have an idea of the first letter, say, but there's a wrong word beginning with that letter at the back of your mind, so you say the wrong word to get it out of the way. Then other words, sound, or syllables come to you and you try them out. After a while, sometimes, you get to the word you wanted (which may be a disappointment). But at each stage, you experience what comes as just coming.

But if you do get the right word, how do you know that it is the right word, that this word is the word that was on the tip of your tongue at the outset? No matter how sure you may feel, no such feeling guarantees the identity; nor need there be conclusive proof that you have got it right. Your evidence, and it is evidence rather than proof, might be that the word that came finally has a property (like a Greek root) that you thought the word you wanted had; but what should perhaps count more is how well you now see this word slide into the sentence you were then making (or, to be Freudian, into a subtext, perhaps surfacing in silent speech, of a trend in your character you have other grounds to think real). What certainly is not true is that at the outset you experienced a muffled mental thing and that you experienced it being, either slowly or all at once, unwrapped.

It is hard not to believe that there are causes responsible for what in our mental life we experience as just coming to us. But it seems that this is a faith, a creed connected with three hundred years of successes elsewhere, not a belief justified by tracing a flow of energy from experienced causes to effects that are those things in our mental lives that we experience as just coming to us.

When we cannot understand knowledge as acquired or justified by experience of its subject matter, our preferred second best (at least as it seems best understood in contemporary philosophy of science) is that it should be the best explanation we can think of for what we do observe; theory is second-best knowledge, and the best contemporary philosophy of science sees the justification of theory as inference to the best explanation. Each of us seems to hold a theory about (at least) the rest of us. You see Alf leave his house at midday and walk toward Bert's café. It seems pretty clear that this is something Alf is doing, an action he is performing, rather than something he is undergoing passively. If Alf were hungry, that is, wanted to eat, and if Alf thought that, all things considered, Bert's café would be the best place to eat now, then what Alf was doing would be an eminently sensible thing to do. So since Alf seems a sensible sort, we conclude that, probably, Alf is hungry and thinks food can be got at Bert's. Some events involving people seem to us to be actions they perform, and we seem to think we have understood people's actions when we can attribute to the agents desires and beliefs it is plausible to suppose them to have because if they did have them, then what they did would be a sensible thing to do. This is the belief–desire theory of action. It was one of Freud's contributions to human understanding to see that certain things we did not formerly think to be actions at all, such as dreams, neurotic symptoms, and slips of the tongue, nevertheless are actions; and to discern, by interpretation, in the agents of those actions beliefs and desires that though themselves not always especially sensible, would nevertheless make those actions seem to their agents sensible things to do, given those beliefs and desires. In this way, Freud was able to explain the fine detail of dreams, neurotic symptoms, and slips of the tongue; and it is not that Freud does so better than his "rivals" but that he has no rivals; no one else explains the fine detail at all. So we have good reason to believe Freud's rich theory of the unconscious.[3]

Notice that Freud has extended our ordinary theory from things that seem obviously to be actions to things we did not formerly think were actions. In this extension, where the explanation appeals to unconscious beliefs and desires, there is no chance (at least before insight in therapy, and that cannot be guaranteed) of experience of those beliefs and desires even in our own case; an argument from analogy with our own unconscious minds to the unconscious minds of others would be a case of the blind leading the blind. But there is nothing special about unconscious beliefs and desires in this point; for the mental states that, on our ordinary theory, explain actions are beliefs and desires. These are fundamentally propositional attitudes, and there is no such thing as an experience of these propositional attitudes in ourselves; so we cannot use an argument from analogy with our own propositional attitudes to justify belief in the propositional attitudes of others.

But then why should we think that anybody has propositional attitudes? Because we think people, including ourselves, do things, and the hypothesis that they have (certain) propositional attitudes is the best explanation we have come up with for why they might do what they do. Tell yourself a story in which we are instructed from childhood to apply the belief–desire theory to people, including ourselves, until, if we are eventually allowed to become more or less independent adults among other more or less independent adults, applying the theory has become second nature to us. If without any prior habituations people could be habituated from childhood to apply Maxwell's theory of electromagnetism, those who managed to grow up might do so believing that they had privileged access to their local region of the electromagnetic field. But vastly more important, it is a considerable confirmation of the belief–desire theory that almost all people can be rather successfully habituated in its thoroughgoing application. Epistemology naturalized is another of Quine's great ideas.[4] At the least, it is the requirement that the truth of no theory we claim to know should be incompatible with our knowing it (as pure mathematics and all theories about very abstract objects can seem to be); and better, for each theory that we claim to know, there should be a good explanation for how we might know it. The fact that the belief–desire theory is confirmed by our ready mastery of it hints that it might be possible to give a good explanation of how we might know that theory; that hint seems promising, for otherwise it is all too natural to wonder whether the theory might not be idle mythology. Each generation habituates the next in the theory of propositional attitudes until the next, by and large, applies it to itself and its successors so smoothly as to be unthinkingly (mostly – analysts do not lack patients); and since each generation's best explanation for the smooth habituation of itself and its successors in the theory is that the theory is true, each generation has reason to believe the theory is true, rather than blind superstition imposed on children by their parents. The later we come in intelligible history, the more reason we have to believe the theory. (What is remarkable is that intelligible history could have got started in the first place; but that is another story.)

But if we do not experience our own propositional attitudes, *how* can we become habituated in applying the theory? We pick out the actions of others, perhaps as events involving them to which they apply the theory, making themselves out as agents of actions; it is important that the theory is such that this can often be done not too implausibly. Then, when we encounter new actions, perhaps by the theory's rules of thumb (possession of which is called a good knowledge of people), we dream up hypothetical beliefs, desires, and doubtless propositional attitudes of other sorts, both intellectual and emotional, to explain those actions. The better known the agent is to us, the more we will already have other hypotheses about his beliefs and desires; and the richer our stock of hypotheses about the agent, the more it will predict actions other than those we have already observed. If we subsequently observe the agent performing those predicted actions, then (on the standard, if defective, hypotheticodeductive model) our hypotheses are confirmed; we are coming to know and understand the agent better. This is how we know ourselves no less than how we know others, except that proximity has the consequence that usually our richest stock of hypotheses is about ourselves (or, as very young children, perhaps about our parents). In part, the therapy of psychoanalysis is a technique for enabling those not as adept as they might be in applying the theory to themselves (which is all of us all of the time) to do so more adeptly.

There is more than a whiff of behaviorism about this picture. (The word "picture" is, in this context, Wittgentein's.) But it is an epistemological, not a metaphysical, behaviorism. That is, our evidence for the theory of propositional attitudes is what we can observe, in the first instance, in others like our parents and, with maturation, in ourselves; and what we observe are actions or, more crudely, bodily movements. But this evidence is best explained by, and thus confirms, the theory of propositional attitudes in others and ourselves. So we have good reason to believe that in others and ourselves there are propositional attitudes, which, according to the theory, are not behavior or (mere) dispositions to it. We are for ourselves theoretical entities.

Metaphysical behaviorism may have been gotten upon epistemological behaviorism by reduction, that is, by identifying the evidence for a theoretical entity with that entity. Reduction is sometimes motivated by an incapacity to understand how we could acquire the concept of an entity we do not and perhaps, as in the case of numbers, cannot experience. But then, we do not understand how we can acquire the concept of an entity we do experience. Ideas are *not* faint copies of impressions; ideas are never images. But having denied Hume, there is nothing explanatory that we know to say about the nature of concepts.

But is it not true that we at least sometimes experience, hear in the mind's ear, silent speech when we think (hard and long about complex or difficult subjects)? Yes. Well, the interlocuter might suggest, perhaps our (occurrent) thoughts just are our silent speeches; so we do experience our thoughts after all. But it is perfectly possible for one's silent speech to be nonsense, like "Twas brillig and the slithy toves did gyre and gimble in the wabe." That silent speech is only into the mind's ear certainly makes it mental, as mental images are to the mind's eye; but it does not make it thought. Although it is not obvious that anything suffices to make it into thought, if anything can do so, then what can is probably just what makes overt, public speech more or less thoughtful.

But what makes speech, silent or overt, thoughtful? That it express thoughts; but thoughts are propositional attitudes and we do not experience them, so what is our evidence that speech, silent or overt, is thoughtful? That it fit into the skein of action around it, including other acts of speaking. What is it to fit into this skein? That the skein continue. The fit need not be entirely felicitous. Suppose he says, "There are less soldiers than officers in that army"; that you reply, "Count nouns are modified by 'few'; 'less' is for mass nouns"; and that he says, "There are fewer soldiers than officers in that army." He made a mistake for which you offered correction, which he accepted; but the skein, even with a brief snarl, continued. It is not clear that it is possible to analyze out, as it were, the concept of a rule. Rules of speech (for example, rules of grammar) seem to be regularities (more or less) of speech embedded in regularities of critical behavior. But this formulation only squeezes what is curious about rules into a curious bulge at which behavior is critical. It might be that critical responses to his nonconformity with the regularity are actions that prompt him toward such conformity, assuming that he is sensitive to such responses and wants to conform, at least enough not to be utterly left out; but it is unclear whether this formulation illegimately presupposes that he can recognize criticism as such. If all it requires of criticism is that it be a response that he does not want and that he is somehow (or by any means at all) acute enough to notice, in the sense that by adjusting his behavior so that it comes to be in fact in conformity with the regularity, he can put a stop to what he does not want, but it is enough for him to do so that he think of his strategy only as a technique for stopping something unpleasant, rather than as following a rule, then the formulation is probably not viciously circular; but the minimum picture of his thought and his critics' sufficient to make their action intelligible is not clear.

For our purposes, the important thing is that the evidence for the thoughtfulness of speech is that it fit into the skein of action around it and that the evidence for fit is that the skein continue. Thinking of public speech, we might recall Quine's dictum: Language is a social art.[5]

. . . language is a practical creation. It may be observed that in all communication between men, certainty comes only from practical acts and from the verification which practical acts give us. *I ask you for a light. You give me a light:* you have understood me.[6]

If one were to put this passage to a student of the philosophy of language in England or America today and to ask him who he thought might have written it, it would not be too surprising if he were to wonder about Wittgenstein and about Quine but hesitate over hints in the style. In fact, it comes from "Poetry and Abstract Thought," an essay published in 1939 by the great French poet Paul Valéry. Valéry has clearly seen that the evidence for communication is that the skein of action continues.

Picturing the skein (which is all we can picture here), it can seem *almost* as if, so long as the skein continues, it does not much matter whether there are thoughts behind but expressed by thoughtful speech. It indeed does not much matter, unless one wants to explain the fact that the skein continues, and why it goes on in the particular ways that it does; but we do think it no less important to understand one another and ourselves than to talk thoughtfully.

Nevertheless and notwithstanding what has gone before, the experience of thoughtful silent speech is more like an experience of thought than any other. The experience of what one says in one's heart is more like an experience of belief than any other, and the experience of one's soul crying out is more like an experience of desire than any other. Wringing out the rhetoric: mature adults typically have reasonably good judgment as to when their considered silent speech expresses a propositional attitude and, when it does, as to what that propositional attitude is. In such typical cases, their experiences of that considered silent speech is more like an experience of that propositional attitude than any other experience; and this is the more true when that silent speech is an action (as opposed to, what can happen, that it seems like something thrust upon one) best explained, in part, by the possession of that propositional attitude. So to approximate to experience

167

of propositional attitudes, one can do no better than experience of considered silent speech.

It furthermore seems that our silent speech is literally located within us. It is neither in our feet nor in our bellies; it is in our heads. It is neither in our napes nor in our noses; it is inside our heads. It seems to one observer to lie roughly midway between his temples, or perhaps a bit lower and farther back, between his ears. At any rate, we shall presume what must inevitably seem a notorious naïvety to some, that our silent speech has a location inside our heads. It seems no more possible to say two things at once in silent speech than to utter two sentences at the same time aloud; so different episodes of silent speech occur at unproblematically determinate and different times. (Could the place of the pineal gland have been Descartes's approximation to the location of silent speech?)

Summing over two approximations (and not allowing oneself to hope that they will cancel out), we may approximate, albeit roughly and crudely, to locating our propositional attitudes. Having made those leaps, make one more. As our propositional attitudes are approximately located in our heads, so the disembodied person's propositional attitudes are approximately located in his phantom head. There is thus a place for his quantity of conviction and, with it, the possibility of genuine flow from energy lost by light through visual experience to belief; that is, it is possible that some of the beliefs of disembodied people be caused by what they see. We may also sharpen an earlier point. You can imagine that although disembodied, you should address yourself in silent speech no less thoughtful or passionate than your present private soliloquies. In that case you would have reason, like your present reason, to attribute to yourself thoughts or passions.[7]

168

12

Action

As, in perception, matter moves the mind, so, in some action, the mind moves matter. To be sure, some actions, like deciding and imagining, lie wholly within the mind, and these will go as smoothly for the disembodied as their having propositional attitudes. But others, like locomotion, which is moving oneself about, and change of attitude, which is moving one's parts about, may seem harder to disembody; and although there would be no impossibility in supposing that disembodiment paralyzes, it would seem lazy or dishonest to do so without at least trying to imagine moving oneself while disembodied.

Our bodily actions are best understood as movements of our bodies or their parts caused by the beliefs and desires that explain those actions of which those bodily movements are manifestations; in bodily action, belief and desire cause, often via a decision, our bodies to move. The grounds for thinking that the relation between beliefs and desires, on the one hand, and bodily actions that they explain, on the other, is causal are the same as the grounds for distinguishing a person's real reasons that are not good from good reasons that are not really his, that is, rationalizations of what he does, by saying that the first, but not the second, causes him to do what he does; no other way to make the distinction clear seems known.

But there are problems of appropriate causation here, too; as veridical visual experience caused by that in virtue of which it is veridical is not sufficient for vision, so the fact that a bodily movement is caused by beliefs and desires that explain it is not sufficient for that movement to be an action. Davidson[1] tells the following story. Suppose that you and he are mountain climbing, that he is leading, and that he wants you to die. He thinks to himself that by letting the rope slip, he can make you fall and be killed, and he decides to do so; but before he can act on his decision, his want, thought, and decision make him so nervous that his hands shake so, and his palms sweat so, that the rope slips and you fall to your death. Here, bodily changes are caused by desires, beliefs, and decisions, but they are not action. In the corresponding perceptual case, we seemed to get some insight by appealing to the standard external carriers of causation, like light in the case of sight, and sound in the case of hearing. But since in the present case there does not seem to be a standard carrier from decisions to nerves and muscles, nothing like our previous suggestion seems possible. Trying,[2] or making an effort, seems to be what is present in action but missing from Davidson's story; but is trying so much a bodily action already as to beg the question? At any rate, this problem seems to be so difficult that we shall now ask leave not to crack our heads against it any further.

How might common sense suppose energy to be conserved along the course of the causation of bodily movements by beliefs and desires? One supposition seems obvious: begin with quantities of conviction and desire; these, or at least the second, will be expended, but the books will be balanced by a part of the kinetic energy manifested in the movements of the body. (Since most of this kinetic energy was presumably stored chemically in the muscles, belief and desire are what we earlier called moving causes of bodily motion.) The quantity of the kinetic energy manifested in the body is, of course, $\frac{1}{2}mv^2$, where v is the speed of the body or its moving part and m its mass.

Now consider transposing into the disembodied mode. If in the disembodied person we suppose a quantity of his desire to move to be lost, we will not be able to balance the books in the same way as we did in the embodied case; for since the disembodied person has no body, he has no mass and therefore can have no kinetic energy. (One might wonder whether these considerations explain why some seem to think locomotion by the disembodied would require truly occult powers.)

If one who is embodied is moved passively from A to B, and he is alert, he will have a continuous view from his successive positions along the way. The stages of his view issue in beliefs as to the nature and array of objects along his route. It is possible that the quantity of conviction of those beliefs should derive entirely from light energy (in the case of sight, which is the sense on which we are now concentrating) impinging on his eyes during his journey. These reflections suggest a construction.

We can imagine that as a disembodied person (successfully) moves himself from A to B, then, first, he is in fact successively at all points along a path from A to B; second, he acquires much the same beliefs via perception as he would have acquired had he been moved passively from A to B; third, he begins his successful journey with a desire to go from A to B that gradually weakens;[3] because, fourth, at various intermediate points along the way, he could go on either through C or through D, and he does in fact go through, say, C rather than D because he wants to go through C; and, fifth, the quantity of conviction of the true belief that he was at C rather than D derives, partly, from his original desire to go from A to B and from his subsidiary desire to go through C rather than D. Thus, when the disembodied person moves himself from A to B, the (generally) true beliefs about the stages of his journey draw their quantity of conviction from two sources. One is the perception of what he experiences, including himself at intermediate points, along the way; the other is the quantity of his desire to make that journey by way of that route. The fact, if we may describe a fiction thus, that there are two sources is connected with a fact about action noted by Elizabeth Anscombe: one (who is now embodied) can know the attitude

171

of his limbs either by observing them or (without observation, as she puts it, which seems to mean) by having satisfied a desire so to dispose them. Thus, were a disembodied person to change the attitude of his phantom body, and so to move himself, while undergoing total sensory deprivation, he would still come to know the new array of his limbs. If conservation of energy is to be satisfied, the quantity of conviction in these new beliefs must come from somewhere, and it cannot *ex hypothesi* come from matter by perception of it. It could satisfy conservation to suppose that it comes from the quantity of his desire to rearrange himself. If we adopt this construction, then the disembodied can move themselves without acting on matter at all. In moving themselves, they will typically acquire beliefs through perception of their passing surroundings; they will thus be acted upon by matter. We embodied people walk by pushing against the ground, thus imparting momentum to it, whence, via Newton's third law of motion, our bodies derive momentum and kinetic energy; we acquire kinetic energy because we are sources of it. But on our construction, a disembodied person does not give up energy to matter by pushing it; he is not (yet) a source of kinetic energy because, having no body and thus no mass, he can have no kinetic energy to surrender. What makes an embodied person's locomotion his action is that the kinetic energy manifested in it derives via trying from, in part, his desire to move. Among the disembodied, the energy of locomotion is not kinetic energy, which *ex hypothesi* it could not be, but rather shows up in (some of) the quantity of conviction of beliefs acquired along the way. Nevertheless, this quantity comes from a quantity of desire to move, as it would were an embodied person with total sensory deprivation to rearrange his limbs and know their new disposition. Indeed, it is easier for the disembodied to move themselves, since they need take no detour through muscle to shift heavy matter like bones; that is, whereas in the embodied, desire can be only that sort of fragment of a total cause that we called a moving cause, desire

172

could be just about all of the cause of successful locomotion by the disembodied.

This construction may seem bizarre to some. Note first that we have spoken only of successful action and as if desire alone were the only source of the energy of action. But what of failure? And isn't action explained by desire *and belief*? But could we not suppose that in a (sane) person, the satisfaction of desire is its exhaustion[4] in successful action, whereas in a sensible person, a quantity of conviction as to means will be exhausted in unsuccessful action?

Next, in addition to walking and shifting our limbs, we embodied people can also move other material objects, for the most part manually; could the disembodied move objects? Some things one does, like lighting one's lighter, one does by doing things like flicking its wheel, and this one does, in part, by moving one's thumb down briskly. But moving one's thumb is not something one does by doing something else. One just does it; it is, in Arthur Danto's term, a basic action.[5] Unless telekinesis is possible, it would seem that the only material objects one can just move, that is, move but not by doing something else, are parts of one's body. Indeed, asked how one knows where one's body stops and the rest of matter begins, it would not be silly to answer that it stops where one's capacity just to move matter gives out. So since the disembodied have no bodies, if they were unable to move material objects, they would be as able to use the instruments at their disposal (namely, none) as we are to use the instruments at our disposal (namely, only our bodies); and it might be unfair to expect more. On the other hand, perhaps we can imagine that when an unattached and not too heavy material object enters the volume occupied by, say, their right phantom hand, it becomes an, as it were, temporary body part (with no counterparts) and they can just move it in whatever way you can just raise your right hand. If so, then if they do not coincide with and manipulate vacant human cadavers too often or too long, perhaps our ghosts could

173

be poltergeists without being embodied. That would be one way in which psychic energy might be able to leave them for more familiar energies in matter like kinetic energy.

This last topic is of some further interest. So long as the disembodied can only absorb energy from matter through perception but can in no way emit energy, it is hard to see how they could do anything but, as it were, grow without ever decaying. It is perhaps in something like this way that Addison's association between the immateriality of the soul and its immortality can seem natural. But it also seems too cheap a proof of the immortality of the soul. So could the disembodied die?

Very roughly, entropy is disorder, and the second law of thermodynamics says that entropy never decreases. (The first law is the conservation of energy.) Death, which is a kind of decay, is an increase in entropy. (Indeed, the death of each living thing may be necessary if the second law is to be consistent with evolution, which seems often to involve changes from less to more complex organizations of matter. An organization of matter is in the relevant way more complex if there are fewer ways it could arise all at once by a random collocation of basic bits of matter. Increasing such complexity seems to decrease entropy; but if inevitable death guarantees that all such increases are only local and temporary, the second law may be true overall and in the large.) So perhaps we could imagine that in addition to being subject to the first law, the disembodied are also subject to the second, that they undergo a constant degradation of psychic energy into, say, radiant heat and that eventually this decay overtakes their growth sufficiently that they die. If that does not beg the question, perhaps they can die (without working themselves to death as poltergeists).

When a disembodied person moves himself, the fact that it is he who is moving himself (rather than, to jest, the ectoplasmic winds pushing him) emerges from the fact that the quantity of his desire to be away is the source of his eventual beliefs about his journey. But because desire lost is balanced[6] by beliefs acquired, it might be wondered whether there will be difficulties about distinguishing real self-locomotion by disembodied people from the illusion or hallucination in them of it. To be sure, a part of this doubt seems to have an easy answer. The disembodied are firmly located in space; initially, we located parts of them by the regions of convergence of the lines of sight of their veridical visual experience; later, we outlined their volumes more substantially by where more familiar forms of energy are lost (the books being balanced at a fixed rate of exchange by quantities of conviction). Their locations are thus objective in the sense that it is possible for their beliefs about where they are to be false; the requisite sense of objectivity is an independence between their believed and their actual place. Their motion, or change of place, is thus equally objective. Typically, then, when a disembodied person has an illusion or a hallucination of moving himself from A to B, the fact that this is an illusion or a hallucination will emerge as the fact that his position has not changed from A to B.

But suppose that at exactly the same time as he is hallucinating, he is blown by the ectoplasmic winds from A to B along exactly the path he thinks he follows. If in both this case and genuine cases of moving himself, psychic energy passes straight from his desire to move to beliefs that he has moved, how will the cases differ? Let us try to think this question through: does the conduit we imagined from desire to belief pass through motion; that is, is a quantity of his desire first converted to motion and only thence into a quantity of (*therefore* true) conviction that he has moved himself? How could it do so unless there is a *quantity* of his motion to be an intermediate receptacle of conserved energy, as there must be in a causal picture of locomotion? This intermediate quantity must not be tactual or kinesthetic experience, at least not pure and simple; for that would threaten the objectivity of his motion. But if we say that it is to be veridical tactual or kinesthetic experience, then we will need, as always, to imag-

175

ine what it might be for that experience to be caused by that in virtue of which it is veridical, which is here his motion. His motion, however, can exhibit no kinetic energy either gained at the expense of his desire to move or lost to his tactual or kinesthetic experience (as) of motion; for having no body, he has no mass and thus can have no kinetic energy.

There seems to be no alternative for this intermediate receptable of energy but his velocity (though there might be analytic reasons to prefer a function of it, like half its square, to his velocity itself). This result can be viewed as a point in favor of dualism. What it seems really to mean is that because disembodied persons have no bodies, they have no inertia to figure in the energy of their motion; the energy of their motion is determined entirely by their velocity. But unlike photons, even great velocity should not enable them to impart motion to matter that they reach, for photons do act thus on matter, and for that reason momentum, and thus a hint of a sort of mass due to motion, has been attributed to photons. We must forbid even a hint of the scandal of mass in the disembodied. But if we too rigidly forbid the disembodied to impart momentum to matter even remotely, we will risk so utterly sealing in their psychic energy as to threaten our imaginary way of killing them off. In order that they be able to die without having bodies, they should be able to shed energy without having mass; we must deny that what can impart momentum remotely must always have mass. In order that they remain totally penetrable by matter (impenetrability by matter being a hallmark of matter), we must insist that they never impart momentum to matter by "colliding" with it. But we may also suppose that psychic energy can degrade into radiant heat (which jiggles molecules it bathes) without forcing mass into disembodied people. Moreover, it even seems consistent to suppose that since poltergeists move material objects inside their phantom bodies not by pushing but by the direct conversion of desire to kinetic energy, poltergeists can move material objects and yet lack physical bodies (except for their temporary body parts). Indeed, we may *be* trapped poltergeists.

Suppose, then, that the energy of a disembodied person's motion is determined entirely by his velocity. Then we can imagine the causal wiring (or some of it) of what it might be for him to move himself to be diagrammed schematically as follows. In successful locomotion from A to B, the quantity of his desire to move from A to B is gradually reduced.[7] At the same time, he acquires a velocity, a speed along the route (or what is left of it) from A to B that he desires to traverse; and there is a fixed rate of conversion between the quantity of desire[8] that he loses and the velocity (or something like half its square) that he acquires. While he is moving, passing through intermediate points like C let us suppose, he loses a fraction of his velocity, he has tactual or kinesthetic experience (as) of moving through C, and he comes to believe that he sent himself through C on his way from A to B. Moreover, there are fixed rates of conversion, first, between the fraction of his velocity lost and the psychic energy of the tactual or kinesthetic experience he has and, second, between the latter quantity and the quantity of his conviction that he sent himself through C (so, canceling out psychic energy in experience, there is a fixed rate of conversion between the fraction of velocity he lost and the quantity of conviction he acquired).

One presumes that some of the conviction about sending himself through C that he thus acquires feeds back, as the jargon has it, into how he subsequently directs his desire into his velocity from C onward toward B. Any lifelike description of such looping should include a detailed description of what we have just now called his directing his desire. Direction in this sense is an agency of the will, the executive function of the mind. Suppose that someone performs an action that is correctly explained by his having certain beliefs and desires and that the explanation correctly mentions that at an intermediate stage, he made a certain effort e. The psychic energy lost from his beliefs and desires eventually will be of a

177

certain total amount l, and he will have expended an amount a in action. In e there will be a certain intermediate (passing) total amount i of psychic energy.[9] Let us assume that in the disembodied, i must equal a; what is spent in action comes wholly from effort. But where does effort come from? One might then speculate whether if l were always equal to i, that would be evidence that the will might be understood causally but that if i were consistently greater than l, that would be evidence that the will is an exception to the conservation of energy, a source of psychic energy that comes out of nothing and thus perhaps is a phenomenon that cannot be fully understood. (We have no guarantee, especially *a priori*, that nature can always be understood. But note that since the second possibility uses an energy flow picture of causation rather than a regularity picture, under the second possibility the will might be uncaused and yet regularly predictable, making it to an extent intelligible.) It would be pleasant thus to add substance to the debate between those who think freedom of the will compatible with a thoroughly determinist understanding of action and those who think the will cannot be free unless it is free of causal determination.

It is only natural to ask how a disembodied person's desire to shift himself from A to B can convert to a velocity from A to B and, part of that, to his registering his shifting himself. We earlier encountered another version of this how-question: how can light energy be converted to the psychic energy of veridical visual experience and, subsequently, to a quantity of conviction? We do not know. We are taught that when matter reflects light, photons arriving at an atom of the matter are sometimes absorbed by the atom's electrons, which for that reason jump to higher energy levels; later, some of these electrons will emit a photon and fall to lower energy levels. How, not why but how, do electrons absorb and emit photons? No one knows; nor is it clear to anyone exactly how it could happen, but we should not abandon our account of reflection for that reason.

Our ignorance of how desire and belief turn into motion, and some motion turns back into belief, should embarrass us neither more nor less than the materialist's ignorance embarrasses him. Can he explain how his desires to move fire up his nerves and muscles? If he is a token–token identity theorist, then (on the most sophisticated version of that theory) his answer is no on principle; he hopes in the glorious future of neurophysiology to explain away the causation of bodily movement by desire. If he is a type–type identity theorist, then his answer is no plus roughly the same pieties about the glorious future of neurophysiology. There is no reason why we should be more embarrassed by our ignorance than he is by his. We may conclude that disembodiment need not paralyze.

Which, if any, are the data against which a piece of philosophy can and should be judged? This seems to be one of the harder philosophical questions, and it may not have a single, a simple, or (one sometimes fears) even any good answer. But in the recent literature, "intuition" often seems to have been used as a term of art for what is taken to be such data; and perhaps that is also part of what was before sometimes meant by "common sense."

It certainly seems common sense that some things that are not actually the case nevertheless could have been. Even if it is obscure how, it seems common sense that our best epistemic access to which unreal things could really have been is through the sensory imagination. No matter exactly how we spell out the detail, it seems common sense that we can imagine being disembodied. If we draw the obvious inference, the conclusion answers to the possibility recorded in the folklore of ghosts. Dualism is the intuitive solution to the mind–body problem.

Notes

1. THE PROBLEM

1 Joseph Addison, *Selections from Addison's Papers Contributed to the Spectator,* ed. Thomas Arnold, Oxford University Press (Clarendon Press), 1891, p. 147.

2 On Descartes, see Bernard Williams, *Descartes: The Project of Pure Enquiry,* Penguin Books, Harmondsworth, 1978, esp. chap. 4; and Margaret Dauler Wilson, *Descartes,* Routledge & Kegan Paul, London, 1978. See also Terence Penelhum, *Survival and Disembodied Existence,* Humanities Press, New York, 1970, esp. the first three chapters; and Saul Kripke, "Identity and Necessity," first published in *Identity and Individuation,* ed. Milton K. Munitz, New York University Press, New York, 1971, pp. 135–64. Kripke argues that because people's mental phenomena could persist even though their bodies vary radically in kind, perhaps even from flesh to metal, their mental phenomena are not necessarily, and thus not actually, identical with phenomena of their bodies. This argument establishes the distinctness between mind and body, not their independence; much as the bodies of Kripke's people vary, they are always embodied. As the hand–fist example shows, distinctness between mind and body is weaker than dualism, independence between mind and body. The last footnote to Kripke's essay makes his appreciation of these points manifest.

2. THE KNOWLEDGE OF POSSIBILITY

1 David Hume, *A Treatise of Human Nature,* ed. L. A. Selby-Bigge, Oxford University Press, 1965, p. 32.

2 This antinomy is analogous to the problem exposited by Paul Benacerraf in "Mathematical Truth," *Journal of Philosophy,* 70 (8 November 1973), 661–79.

3 Isaiah Berlin, "Empirical Propositions and Hypothetical Statements," *Mind,* 59 (July 1950), 289–312.

4   Immanuel Kant, *The Critique of Pure Reason*, trans. Norman Kemp Smith, Macmillan, New York, 1963, B3, p. 43.

5   See John E. Brigham, trans., *The Graphic Work of M. C. Escher*, Hawthorn Books, New York, 1960, pp. 67, 72, 74–6.

6   José A. Benardete, *Infinity*, Oxford University Press (Clarendon Press), 1964, pp. 236–7.

7   For Newton's statement of his argument, see Bernard Lovell, *Emerging Cosmology*, Columbia University Press, New York, 1981, pp. 104–5. But D. W. Sciama states on p. 101 of *Modern Cosmology* (Cambridge University Press, 1971) that Newton discovered difficulties in applying his theory to an infinite system, though Sciama cites nothing from Newton's writings.

8   For more on the issues raised in this chapter, though in another context, see W. D. Hart, "Imagination, Necessity and Abstract Objects," in *Studies on Frege*, ed. Matthias Schirn, vol. 1, Friedrich Frommann Verlag, Stuttgart, 1976, pp. 161–92.

3.   MORE ON IMAGINATION AND MODALITY

1   The interlocutor in this section is from a private communication. The interested reader of this section might like to consult Sydney Shoemaker, "On an Argument for Dualism," in *Knowledge and Mind*, ed. Carl Ginet and Sydney Shoemaker, Oxford University Press, 1983, pp. 233–58; Sydney Shoemaker and Richard Swinburne, *Personal Identity*, Blackwell, Oxford, 1984; and Thomas Nagel, *The View from Nowhere*, Oxford University Press, 1986, p. 42.

2   Arthur Pap, "Logical Nonsense," *Philosophy and Phenomenological Research*, 9 (1948), 269–83; idem, "Are All Necessary Propositions Analytic?" *Philosophical Review*, 58 (1949), 299–320; idem, *Elements of Analytic Philosophy*, Macmillan, New York, 1949, chap. 16b; Hilary Putnam, "Reds, Greens, and Logical Analysis," *Philosophical Review*, 65 (1956), 206–17; Arthur Pap, "Once More: Colors and the Synthetic a Priori," *Philosophical Review*, 66 (1957), 94–9; Hilary Putnam, "Red and Green All Over Again: A Rejoinder to Arthur Pap," *Philosophical Review*, 66 (1957), 100–3.

3   J. L. Austin, "A Plea for Excuses," reprinted in *Philosophical Papers*, ed. J. O. Urmson and G. J. Warnock, Oxford University Press, 1961, pp. 132–3.

4   See W. V. Quine, "Ontological Relativity," in *Ontological Relativity and Other Essays*, Columbia University Press, New York, 1969, pp. 26–68.

5   See Bertrand Russell, *The Problems of Philosophy*, Oxford University Press, 1912, chaps. 8–10.

6   See the essay cited in note 4, Chapter 2.

7   In addition to "Identity and Necessity" cited in note 2, Chapter 1, see Saul Kripke, *Naming and Necessity*, Blackwell, Oxford, 1980. In neither place does Kripke assert either Cartesian dualism or Descartes's argument for dualism.

8   See, for example, George S. Boolos and Richard C. Jeffrey, *Computability and Logic*, 2d ed., Cambridge University Press, 1980, p. 200.

9   W. V. Quine, "Reference and Modality" and "Quantifiers and Propositional Attitudes," reprinted in *Reference and Modality*, ed. Leonard Linsky, Oxford University Press, 1971, pp. 17–34, 101–11.

10 David Kaplan, "Quantifying In," reprinted in *Reference and Modality*, ed. Leonard Linsky, Oxford University Press, 1971, pp. 112–44.

11 Brian Loar, "Reference and Propositional Attitudes," *Philosophical Review*, 81 (1972), 43–62.

4. THE SENSES, PART I

1   Norman Malcolm, *Dreaming*, Routledge & Kegan Paul, London, 1959, chap. 3.

2   J. L. Austin, *Sense and Sensibilia*, ed. G. J. Warnock. Oxford University Press (Clarendon Press), 1962, lecture 5.

3   H. P. Grice, "The Causal Theory of Perception," reprinted in *Perceiving, Sensing and Knowing*, ed. Robert J. Swartz, Doubleday, New York, 1965, pp. 438–72.

5. CAUSATION

1   Nelson Goodman, *Fact, Fiction and Forecast*, Bobbs-Merrill, Indianapolis, Ind., 1965, chap. 2.

2   Ibid., chap. 1.

3   See, for example, Richard P. Feynman, *QED*, Princeton University Press, Princeton, N.J., 1985.

4   See P. M. Harman, *Energy, Force and Matter*, Cambridge University Press, 1982.

5   W. V. Quine, *The Roots of Reference*, Open Court, La Salle, Ill., 1973, pp. 4–8.

6   This issue is discussed a bit more in W. D. Hart, "Causation and Self-Reference," in *Papers on Language and Logic*, ed. Jonathan Dancy, Keele University Library, n.d., pp. 71–87, and reprinted in *Self-Reference:*

Reflections, ed. Steven J. Bartlett and Peter Stuber, Nijhoff, Dordrecht, 1987, pp. 179–92.

7   W. V. Quine, "Necessary Truth," reprinted in *The Ways of Paradox*, Random House, New York, 1968, pp. 48–56.

6. QUANTITY

1   John von Neumann and Oskar Morgenstern, *The Theory of Games and Economic Behavior*, 2d ed., Princeton University Press, Princeton, N.J., 1947, chap. 3 and app.

2   Once a $q: A \rightarrow R$ has been fixed, it can be extended to supersets B of A on which E remains an equivalence relation by requiring that for any x in B, $q(x) = a$ iff $q(y) = a$ for some y in A such that xEy. This is important insofar as axiom 14 requires that the members of A exhibit no "chemistry" under m, to which extent we may want a way to extend q to things outside A that would "react" with members of A, or with each other, under m.

3   I. N. Herstein and John Milnor, "An Axiomatic Approach to Measurable Utility," *Econometrica*, 21 (April 1953), 291–7.

7. DESIRE

1   Alfred F. MacKay, *Arrow's Theorem: The Paradox of Social Choice*, Yale University Press, New Haven, Conn., 1980, chap. 3.

2   For discussions of transitivity of preference, see, in addition to MacKay's book, R. Duncan Luce and Howard Raiffa, *Games and Decisions*, Wiley, New York, 1957; and Gordon Tullock, *Toward a Mathematics of Politics*, University of Michigan Press, Ann Arbor, 1967.

8. BELIEF

1   Leonard J. Savage, *The Foundations of Statistics*, 2d ed., Dover, New York, 1972, especially chaps. 2 and 3.

2   Peter Unger, "I Do Not Exist," in *Perception and Identity: Essays Presented to A. J. Ayer with His Replies to Them*, ed. G. F. MacDonald, Macmillan, New York, 1979, pp. 235–51.

3   The example, but not the claims about it here criticized, comes from Martin Gardner's "Mathematical Games" column in the *Scientific American* for December 1970; Gardner credits the example to Bradley Efron.

1 Donald Davidson, "Actions, Reasons, and Causes" and "Freedom to Act," reprinted in *Essays on Actions and Events,* Oxford University Press, 1980, pp. 3–19, 63–81.

2 This construction is clearly too crude in at least one respect: it implies that in pure wishful thinking, desire would wane as belief waxes; but it is hardly the usual desire that wanes merely as one acts in order to satisfy it. Here a distinction may be useful. It is a familiar fact that one often decides which of one's desires to seek to satisfy. Decision being an executive function traditionally assigned to the will, this familiar fact suggests (as Plato saw) that we distinguish the will from the reservoir of desire. The will is also traditionally conceived as a sort of well from which effort springs. So we might change the construction as follows. While one is acting in order to satisfy a desire, psychic energy flows not from that desire, but from the will; then if the action succeeds, the psychic energy of that desire replenishes the will, the exhaustion of the desire being its satisfaction. This change in the construction requires a quantity peculiar to effort and the will. The quantity of trying suggested in note 9, Chapter 12, might fill the bill.

3 Davidson, "Mental Events," in *Essays on Actions and Events,* pp. 207–25.

4 Compare W. V. Quine, "Mind and Verbal Dispositions," in *Mind and Language,* ed. Samuel Guttenplan, Oxford University Press (Clarendon Press), 1975, pp. 83–95, esp. the paragraph third from the end.

5 It has been asked how, if dualism were true, the mind could have evolved. Presuming that life evolved from matter and that the mind evolved from life, one might wonder how what has evolved ultimately from matter could have ceased to depend for its existence on matter. Of course, the presumption might be false. Perhaps mind did not come *from* matter at all; perhaps neither came from anything else at all. A dualist might advocate even that much symmetry between mind and matter; is the question where matter came from any less a stumper than the question where mind came from?

But if we make the presumption for a bit, it seems natural to suppose that life evolved capacities to register its environment, including itself, in various ways. When matter becomes so complexly patterned as to seek to understand not only itself, but also its understanding of itself and its capacity to do so, then perhaps we can obscurely imagine, or at least suppose, that the particular cases of the pattern might cease to depend for their existence on matter of which their ancestors were only arrays. By "cases of the pattern" are meant neither the pattern itself,

184

which is an abstract universal, nor the bodies of patterned protoplasm, which are as physical as rocks, but as Plato saw, an intermediate in kind between abstract objects like numbers and material objects like stones; minds are meant. (Note that energy, too, is intermediate in kind between abstract entities, like the purely geometric form of a river's course, and material stuff, like water.)

The mind emerges, to use Bergston's word, from matter by becoming an artifact of an understanding of itself. One would like an analogy here, such as Israel persisting through the Diaspora or a fictional character acquiring a life of his own beyond the stories his creator originally told about him, but no analogy seems adequate and one despairs of making these notions less paradoxical by any analogy.

10. THE SENSES, PART II

1 We might begin to approximate to one quantity in visual experience by considering these two binary propositional attitudes:

> It looks to i more as if x than as if y,

and

> It looks to i as much as if x as if y.

Hearing, taste, smell, and touch might correspond to replacing looking by sounding, tasting, smelling, and feeling in this impersonal passive construction. We might be able to mix here as we did for belief, letting i look at the wheels of fortune; for other senses, like hearing or touch, we should make the divisions of the wheels sound or feel different, and let i listen to or feel them.

A central difficulty here is that the second relation will probably not be uniformly transitive. If the difference in color between a and b, and between b and c, is less than i can detect visually but that between a and c is not, it may look to i as much as if a is red as if b is red, and as much as if b is red as if c is red, but look more to i as if a is red than as if c is red. Let us call the proposition that b is red intransitive fuzz and, in the first instance, exclude intransitive fuzz from the domains of the two binary propositional attitudes. Nevertheless, to the extent that there are largish sets of propositions on which the second attitude is reflexive, symmetric, and transitive and which have relatively little intransitive fuzz at their edges, then the two propositional attitudes, even with reduced domains, might determine an interesting quantity, call it v, in visual experience.

Could v be extended to any of the intransitive fuzz? If i notices the

185

intransitivity, he would be sensible to be surer that a is red than that b is red, and surer that b is red than that c is red. Indeed, he might be surer that a is red than that a is not red, and surer that c is not red than that c is red. Let c be i's quantity of conviction, and suppose that there is a quantitative law of belief and sight, $c(p) = a \cdot v(p)$ for some constant a of proportionality, which holds where c and v are both defined. When the proposition that p (for example, that b is red) is intransitive fuzz, when c is defined on p, and when, for each r in the domain of v such that $v(r) = c(p)/a$, it looks to i as much as if p as if r, then we might extend v to p by setting $v(p)$ equal to $c(p)/a$.

For the purposes of the text to which this note is appended, the crucial supposition is that when events by virtue of which it is true that p cause the conformation of light that loses energy at the region of convergence of a disembodied person's lines of sight, there is a fixed rate of conversion between the amount of energy the light thus loses and the amount by which his quantity $v(p)$ is increased or sustained and, of course, a quantitative law of belief and sight.

2 In a steam locomotive, coal is burned and electrochemical energy is converted thereby finally to the kinetic energy of the train's motion. Should we say that there is here one basic sort of energy that takes successive forms, or two interconvertible sorts of energy? The question seems moot. But energy apart, the things, minds and bodies (like coal and trains), remain distinct. Indeed, minds and bodies can occupy identical regions of space and so by Locke's principle must be things of different kinds. That dualism of minds and bodies seems more important than a dualism or monism of energy.

3 Some suggest that sensations are intensional and that they represent parts of the body as disordered. It is distinctive of perceptual experience to represent; a visual image of a gashed leg represents a leg as gashed. By and large, different perceptual experiences represent different contents. Does an itch in the left shoulder or a headache represent the shoulder or the head as in a certain state? If distinctly, then the first seems to represent the shoulder as itching, and the second, the head as hurting; so there is not something other than the sensation that it represents as present in the shoulder or head. If the itch and the ache each represent the shoulder and the head as disordered, that is, as in the same state, then they seem inadequately representative perceptions and perhaps so impoverished that it would be more enlightening not to classify them with perceptions. (Do sensations of orgasm represent the genitals as disordered?)

4 See note 1, Chapter 3.

5 We are familiar only with minds that, as it happens, are embodied. For all

one knows for sure, there may be some disembodied minds about, though no one knows of any good reason to think so. So suppose that in fact people do not become disembodied. Someone might ask why. This is a scientific question, and perhaps there is no particular reason that a philosopher should have the correct answer to an empirical question.

By and large, electrons occur around protons and vice versa; we say there is a force of attraction between them. Similarly, it seems that the quarks in a proton in some sense cannot be isolated. So perhaps there is reason to suppose something like a force of attraction between minds and, say, complex living organisms. Or perhaps disembodied minds so much want to be embodied that they occupy vacant infant bodies (which causes thorough amnesia), and thus minds are disembodied only very briefly. Or perhaps the energy input to a disembodied mind is at most too small to sustain mental activity, so all disembodied people wane quickly into death.

11. PROPOSITIONAL ATTITUDES

1 See W. D. Hart, "Models of Repression," in *Philosophical Essays on Freud*, ed. Richard Wollheim and James Hopkins, Cambridge University Press, 1982, pp. 180–202.

2 Terence Penelhum twice (*Survival and Disembodied Existence*, Humanities Press, New York, 1970, pp. 21, 49) denies, without stating a reason, that the disembodied could sleep.

3 See Richard Wollheim, *Sigmund Freud*, Viking, New York, 1971.

4 W. V. Quine, "Epistemology Naturalized," in *Ontological Relativity and Other Essays*, Columbia University Press, New York, 1969, pp. 69–90.

5 W. V. Quine, *Word and Object*, Technology Press, Cambridge, Mass.; Wiley, New York, 1960, p. ix.

6. Paul Valéry, *The Art of Poetry*, Pantheon Books, New York, 1958, p. 64.

7 For a bit more on issues related to those considered in this chapter, see W. D. Hart, "The Anatomy of Thought," *Mind*, 92 (1983), 264–9.

12. ACTION

1 Donald Davidson, "Freedom to Act," reprinted in *Essays on Actions and Events*, Oxford University Press, 1980, p. 79.

2 See Jennifer Hornsby's *Actions*, Routledge & Kegan Paul, London, 1980, for a good treatment of the role of trying in action.

3 There is a crudity here that we have encountered before; see note 2, Chapter 9.

4 Ibid.
5 Arthur Danto, "What We Can Do," *Journal of Philosophy*, 60 (1963), 435–45; idem, "Basic Actions," *American Philosophical Quarterly*, 2 (1965), 141–8.
6 See note 3.
7 Ibid.
8 Ibid.
9 There may be a quantity of trying to be founded in

> *i* tries harder to bring it about that x than to bring it about that
> y; and
> *i* tries as hard to bring it about that x as to bring it about that
> y,

where $m(a, x, y)$ sets *i*'s objective, with probability a, as being the case that x and, with probability $1 - a$, that y. The idea is that trying is intermediate between belief and desire, on the one hand, and action, on the other. The quantity of trying ultimately expended in action might exactly balance the quantity of desire (ultimately) expended in that (successful) action. If the books thus balance, conservation is met, so we may have a causal picture of action. But since conservation is not a necessary truth, it is not a necessary truth that the books will balance; as it were, more trying might come out of the will than could have been bled off desire. If one can thus simply create energy *ex nihilo*, that would perhaps be a variety of what is sometimes called contracausal freedom of the will and may be connected with some ideas of agent causation.

Index

action, 169–77
  basic, 173
  belief–desire model of, 162
  locomotion, 169, 174
Addison, Joseph, 7, 174
analyticity, 31
Anscombe, Elizabeth, 171
a posteriori knowledge of necessity, 26,
  34–40, 48–9
Aristotle, 4, 131
Austin, John, 31, 52

belief, 102–26
  and gambling, 108–12
  transitivity of comparative sureness,
  105–8
Benardete, José, 18
Berkeley, George, 13
Berlin, Isaiah, 12
Boolean algebra, 114–15

causation, 8, 45–6, 59–68, 128
  and action, 169
  and conservation of energy, 62–8,
  69, 131, 152, 178
  and perception, 11, 55–8, 136
  moving, 67, 170, 172
  problem of appropriate, 56–8, 159–
  70
conception, 15
consciousness, 153–4

Danto, Arthur, 173
Davidson, Donald, 128, 133–4, 170
death, 6, 174, 176
de dicto possibility, 27, 32, 40–3, 144
dependence, 1–8, 11, 23, 43, 175
Descartes, René, 1–8, 51, 62, 130–2,
  143
desire, 89–101

  and action, 130
  and expected utility, 96–8
  and gambling, 95–8
  interpersonal comparisons of utility,
  99
  transitivity of indifference, 92
  transitivity of preference, 93–4
  zeros and units, 98–101

epistemology naturalized, 163
error and perception, 15
Escher, M. C., 17
evolution, 184–5 n5
explanation, 12
  inference to the best, 12–13, 21, 29,
  33, 161
exportation, 41

Feynman, Richard, 63
Freud, Sigmund, 127, 132

Galois, Evariste, 16, 22
gender, 142–3
ghosts, 143–4, 147, 149–50, 173
  and common sense, 179
Gödel, Kurt, 16
Goodman, Nelson, 61
Grice, H. P., 54, 57

hearing, 138–9
Helmholtz, Hermann von, 63, 132
Herstein, I. N., 75
Hobbes, Thomas, 16
Hume, David, 9, 33, 55, 59–62, 66,
  155, 165

idealism, 13
identity, 2–4, 38–9
  personal, 42, 144–7
imagination, 9–22, 23–49

For EU product safety concerns, contact us at Calle de José Abascal, 56–1°,
28003 Madrid, Spain or eugpsr@cambridge.org.